Sevren

MW00445389

May my story
bless your life

Lakisha Davis-Small

lakishadavissmall@gmail

"Your Deliverance Is Coming!"

202-421-2311

Your Deliverance is Coming

LAKISHA N. DAVIS-SMALL

Your Deliverance Is Coming

Copyright © 2014 by Lakisha N. Davis-Small

ALL RIGHTS RESERVED. No part of this book may be reproduced or transmitted in any form without the expressed written consent from the author. This book is designed to inspire, encourage, engage, and educate its readers in the area of brokenness, rape, domestic violence, and healing. It is sold with the understanding that the author is not engaged in rendering legal or medical services. If assistance is needed in these areas, the services of a competent professional should be sought.

The author shall have neither liability nor responsibility to any person, or entity with respect to any loss or damage caused, or alleged to have been caused, directly or indirectly, by the material in this book. Some of the names are real, and some are fiction.

ISBN-10: 0-692-02108-6
ISBN-13: 978-0-692-02108-8

LCCN: 2014906363

Scripture taken from The Message unless otherwise noted. Copyright © 1993, 1994, 1995, 1996, 2000, 2001, 2002. Used by permission of NavPress Publishing Group.

Printed in the United States of America

CONTENTS

DEDICATION

This book is dedicated first to God, and secondly, to my grandmother, Mittie Lee Norman (1919-1989).

My grandmother is truly missed, and this book is a symbol of my appreciation for the love that she has shown me. My grandmother died when I was ten years old, so for the first ten years of my life, I walked with my grandmother, talked with her, and learned her ways. She was from LaGrange, North Carolina and had the southern hospitality that people see in me when they enter my home or my heart. I would sit in the kitchen with her while she cooked.

At her funeral, I sang an inspirational song that mimicked what she meant to me. She was truly my angel, and I felt it. Her loving touch and spirit were as sweet as pumpkin pie. My grandmother also taught my Dad how to show love and that is why I know he loves me.

ACKNOWLEDGMENTS

God, thank you for your favor, love, and mercy over my life; and for guiding me to write this book.

Thank you Daddy, for always believing in all of my dreams. We know it doesn't stop here.

Thank you to the young lady that touched my hand at my friend's church. You told me that God said, "Keep writing." I would also like to thank the young lady, who acted as an angel in disguise and shared with me the ineffectiveness of procrastination. Her words sparked an inner fire, which prompted me to complete this book.

Thank you! You know who all of you are. Thanks to those who have always had my back through adversity, especially those who have worked closely with me through the years. You showed me how much you care.

Thanks to my husband David and daughter Serenity for your loving support and allowing me to bring this book to completion.

Thank you reader, for getting to know me.

INTRODUCTION

Lakisha Davis, a young woman from the historic inner city area of Shaw, Washington, D.C. My courageous fight for survival is amazing. I was exposed to crime, murder, and hustling, for the majority of my life, yet my father made sure that God was the foundation of my being. A church girl my entire life, I struggled while battling two different worlds, spiritual and worldly—a world in which I believe Angels and Demons exist. Living with the pain and shame of my horrific past caused my faith to grow weary many times in my young adult life. However, my faith would never completely die even when I felt like a sheep amongst wolves, or that my brokenness extended beyond the break.

My story is remarkable!

I grew up with my father and his family. He stood by my side through the most horrible experiences that occurred in my life, even from the pain of my mother dropping me off in Virginia with my aunt and disappearing at the tender age of five. My mother didn't return until years later. While living with my aunt, my father found me a few months later and brought me back to live with him. While living with my father, I was raped by a distant cousin who was babysitting me, and my other young cousins; all of this happened within the same year! I lived in a family community and couldn't believe this crime was happening within the confinements of my own family. God and my Dad was there to comfort and help me through my beginning stages of healing.

In our neighborhood, everybody cared for one another's children in whatever way they could, whether it was a meal, or an ear to listen, or someone to protect you. There was a mixture of the good, the bad, and the indifferent in the neighborhood of Fifth & Q Street N.W. I will never forget how the environment I grew up in, despite the horrific ordeal I faced as a child, helped to shape the woman I am today.

I often thought about my mom. Seventeen years later, I put my faith to practice and found my Mom whom I had not seen since I was five years old. I never stopped praying for my mom's return, and one day God answered my prayer of faith. Prayer has played a strong factor in my survival. Without the strength of God, I would have given up a long time ago. The pain I felt had to be released, and poetry became my first avenue. I became a poet known as "Smiley" in the Shaw community. I started out at the Bohemian Caverns, a place that famous artists would visit after their performance. When I recited my poetry, my finishing line would be, *"My name is Smiley because I am gifted enough to smile through my adversity!"* Doors of opportunity opened, one, which led to an appearance on WHUR 96.3 Spoken Word at Joe's Place. I performed at the DuPont Circle for the Take Back the Night Rally, with the D.C. Rape Crisis Center, with WPGC 95.5, and Channel 9 News.

Yet, there still was a storm brewing in my heart as I continued to strive for greatness and not give in to the emotional pain that continued to haunt me. I lived in a world that I didn't choose, but managed to use my pain to be inspired, and to inspire others. Still, I kept moving forward. In life, I felt I was kicked around. Although, down many times, I refused to give up! My tears made me stronger, and my prayers kept me focused on my purpose; which was **not** to be abused. Domestic violence became an issue for me in my early 20's.

In my quest for mental freedom, I began to research my history as an African American. What I discovered was the endurance of my people during slavery. The years of slavery became my passion and driving force to keep me striving forward in the midst of my mental slavery from the pain of my past. The power I found from my ancestors during their adversity was amazing! I read many stories captured from former slaves on the *Federal Writers Project* website and still read different ones today. I felt that if they had enough power to persevere through brutality, have their children taken from them and brutally raped on a daily basis, then I could be a type of Harriet Tubman myself, and lead I and others to emotional freedom.

"If you don't know your past you are doomed to repeat it!"—George
Santayana (December 16, 1863, Madrid –
September 26, 1952, Rome)

CHAPTER 1

Life without My Mother

*I*t all started on the twenty-fourth of January, 1979, at Howard University Hospital in Washington, D.C. Push… push… it's a girl and her name is Lakisha Norman Davis; my middle name is my Dad's last name. That was the day my mother had longed for. She wanted a baby girl, someone to love and someone who would love her back with no strings attached. My Mom believed I could help her forget the painful memories of her past. My mother was twenty-three; my Dad was thirty, and well seasoned in the streets; something my mother wasn't ready for. She was born in rural Virginia and was naïve about city street life and unaware of the danger that lie ahead. My mother and I were like two peas in a pod. She would always take me to the playground. We went often and now, in my adulthood, I still like to go. I'm sure that when I'm a senior I will still go and get on the swings—my favorite attraction at the playground. When I'm on the swings, I feel as free as a bird soaring through the air.

I remember my Mom would take me to the Shaw Clinic, located next to the Shaw Junior High School in Northwest, Washington, D.C. to ensure that she was properly taking care of my health and my dental needs. I remember being happy with her no matter what, or where, we were. She was my mom, and I loved her just the way she expected me to, unconditionally, with no strings attached. I knew that she loved me too. I could feel it deep within me, and she showed me often. My Dad loved me too, but he worked often, so I spent most of my time with my mom. My Dad said when I was two years old, and he had to leave for work, I would cry, "No! No! No! G. Dough. G. Dough meaning "don't go." He responded, "I have to GO meaning, "go." He worked so much, and I missed him. I love him.

My parents lived together on Park Road, located in Washington, D.C., and I still remember how the apartment looked. When you walked into the house, the kitchen was to the left. Oh, the aroma of the Steakumm's that she cooked. The living room was straight ahead, and our bedroom was to the left, which had an en-suite bathroom. God has allowed me to remember things from the age of four until now. Due to my Dad working so many hours, my mother longed for a listening ear and tender loving care. My Dad was absent in the *loving my Mom* department, and I was there to witness it. I remember on one occasion my Mom and Dad were arguing, but I had enough. I grabbed both of their hands. "Don't fight!" I shouted. I was able to calm the storm for a moment but only a moment. A bigger storm was brewing, and it was on its way to our address.

One day my Mom went out with my favorite aunt, Willie Lee. She is my Dad's sister; they went to a nightclub located in Washington, D.C. Aunt Willie Lee wanted to get my Mom out of the house to have some fun; she wanted to alleviate my moms' stress due to my Dad not being home. Therefore, off they went to glide across the dance floor. My Mom was enjoying herself when the devil, I mean, Hugo, introduced himself to her. He gave my Mom his telephone number and asked her to call him. She explained her living situation, and he said that he didn't mind; he just wanted to be her friend. So he said.

My Mom began discussing her personal problems to Hugo, and he provided a listening ear. Eventually, he captured my mom's heart and showed her tender loving care. My Mom and I started spending the night at his house. I was confused. I saw more of this man than I did my Dad, but I didn't say a word. I loved my mom, and whatever she liked, I liked. What I am sharing next really hurt me.

Hugo failed to mention to my Mom at the beginning of their friendship that he was a drug dealer, and he turned my Mom out. I was with her when it got really bad. My Dad knew nothing about this. I held the secret for many years. When I entered adulthood, I told him; he was livid. He tried to remain calm by telling a joke, implicating my premature exposure to life in the fast lane.

I felt my Mom was being defeated by the devil. In my opinion, the enemy was Hugo, and he was out to destroy my mom. I saw my Mom struggle with many things while she was influenced by the wicked influences of this world, but I never stopped loving her, and I never will. My Dad worked so much that he didn't notice my Mom had become pregnant in the midst of all of this foolishness. My Mom was still living with my Dad; she was leading a double lifestyle, which he had no clue about, and now she was pregnant. My Dad found out when my Mom was nine months pregnant—no joke! My Mom was fast asleep when my Dad came home. She would sleep on her side, facing the wall, so my Dad wouldn't notice the pregnancy.

I will never forget one cold December morning in 1984, my Mom and I walked into Howard University Hospital emergency room and, as soon as my Mom reached the information desk, she collapsed onto the floor. I cried, "Mommy, Mommy," while the nurses lifted her and placed her on a stretcher. Fear gripped me at that moment. A security guard approached me and asked if I wanted a sandwich or an apple. I said, "No, thank you. My mommy told me that I can't take food from strangers." Shortly thereafter, my grandma picked me up, my Dad's mom; she was my other favorite person in the world. My Mom gave birth to a baby boy and his father disappeared. My Mom decided it was time to move to her hometown. She gathered me and my brother, packed a few things and moved us to the countryside of Virginia.

We were taken to her mother's house. I was five years old, and my brother was about a month old. My grandmother didn't want to be bothered with me, but she wanted my brother. I believe she didn't want a reminder of her daughter around. She didn't raise my mother. All three of us look alike and seeing me stirred up too many of her emotions. Those were the conclusions I came to. My grandfather raised my Mom just as my father raised me. To my surprise, my Aunt Peaches took me away. I didn't know what was happening. My Mom said that she needed to take care of some things, and she would be right back to get me. I believed her because she always kept her promises. My aunt was married with two children. For a while, I thought they belonged to the devil because they were so mean to me.

They had bunk beds; the boy slept at the bottom and the girl at the top. They both were five to seven years older than I was. My female cousin made me ball up at the end of the bed, and I slept as if I was inside a box, and my male cousin would jab me with stickpins while I tried to sleep. I wanted my Mom so badly; I just knew that she was coming back to get me.

I saw and experienced many things living there that I will never forget. In retrospect, I know my Mom made the best decision she could because she wasn't well; she succumbed to the life that the serpent put before her. My mother's desires for the street were greater than her responsibility—Me!

Lord behold, my knight in shining armor came to rescue me. My Dad! He found out where I was living, by obtaining information from my aunt, and he came to Virginia to get me. I still remember the look on his face when he saw me. I was so happy to see him. He and his buddy picked me up. On our way home, we stopped at Chesapeake Seafood for dinner. My Dad still laughs today when we mention this part of the story. He asked me if I wanted some fish, and I replied, "No, Daddy, please no fish!" I had eaten fish every day in the countryside of Virginia; for breakfast, lunch, and dinner, or so it seemed.

When we arrived in D.C., we lived with my grandma. My Dad went to court to get full custody of me to prevent my Mom from taking me away. That was a painful and embarrassing process because my Dad had to put all of her business out there, and it made her look bad; he didn't lie, but it was hurtful. I have been with my Dad ever since.

My Dad and I had some very adventurous moments. He took me to the Easter egg hunts at the National Zoo in D.C., and we would take subway trips to Reagan National Airport to watch the planes take off right from the platform of the subway. We would sit on a bench and eat snacks that he always packed for us. It is funny because he would pack snacks when we went to the movies too. I still remember my Dad's bike with the extra seat attached. It was our transportation to everywhere. If I weren't riding his shoulders, I was on the back of that bike. My Dad was a vendor, so we were always out in the street, meeting all kinds of people.

My Dad took me to church so much that it would be impossible for me to deny knowing about God and who He really is. Church was seventy-five percent of my life. I was in the choir, enrolled in Bible studies, vacation Bible school; you name it; I was in it. I felt like a church girl because my life was so consumed with church. Being overwhelmed, I began to rebel. My Dad didn't see the rebellion. It was in secret.

My Dad made a way out of no way. He did the best he could do for me, and I truly love him for that. There are two sides to him as there are with many people; one side was fun, eventful, and full of love. My Dad always hugged me and told me that he loved me. However, the other side of my Dad was militant and frustrated sometimes. I remember witnessing a fight and afterwards sitting at the table and conversing with him about it. He said, "Lakisha, if you see somebody fighting what should you do?" I looked at him puzzled because I didn't know. He then preceded, "Tell whoever you are with that your Dad said 'I have to leave!' You know, if I find out that you were watching a fight, we are going to have it out. Lakisha people died from watching fights, and I don't ever want you to get hurt from watching one." My Dad knew he had to guide me spiritually and teach me street sense. Even though I was a church girl, I grew up with crime all around me.

I wouldn't have made it through some of the rough times without my best friend, Shaun. God made sure that we met at five years old, and we have remained friends. Shaun has always been my emotional support system. She was there for me and loved me with all of her heart. She would say, "Kisha, I love you." Shaun said this repeatedly without hesitation, but I couldn't. I was still hurting from my mother's abandonment, but that never discouraged her from speaking from her heart.

The extent of her loyalty was the mark of a true friend. On one occasion, Shaun spent the night with me. It was a cold winter night, and our heating gas was cut off. I was fourteen years old, and my Dad's health kept him admitted back and forth in Howard University. Shaun was the sister I needed to weather the storm with me. For some reason, I don't understand why blood sisters sometimes can't display that same love. I had to go there for a quick moment. She was there with me through all of life's storms. Only a true friend would stay with me in a cold house.

Where was my mom? I still missed her dearly. Let me share with you how it feels to grow up without a mother. Being a daddy's girl wasn't easy, men are logical, and women are emotional, at least in my opinion. I felt an emotional void that only a Mom could fill. Girls need their mother to nurture them, to fill their inner emotions. I stopped receiving that at the age of five.

Please understand me. When my Mom was there, she was good to me, as I remember. However, growing up without her took a serious toll on me. It had a serious effect on my life as an adolescent, and it continues to affect my adulthood. I wasn't what you would call feminine, because I wasn't given the proper education or told that a lady should chew with her mouth closed. I lost my grandma at age ten, so I missed the things a young girl needed to know. I remember when I was in the fourth grade,

I had gone to school without wearing any deodorant; my hair was all over the place, and my clothes were wearing me. I must have prepared for school in the dark. When I arrived, everyone gossiped about me.

"Where was her dad?" some may ask. He didn't see me leave the house. He had enough common sense not to allow me to leave like that. If he had seen how I looked, he would have sent me up to my room until I got myself together.

My school, Scott Montgomery Elementary School, was on the corner from my house, so close that school started at 8:00 a.m. and I could leave at 7:55 a.m. and arrive at class on time. I was rough, and I loved to play with the boys too, not because I was fresh but because I was very energetic. I remember some boys and me on my street participating in a bike race. I was going full speed ahead. When I slammed on the front brakes, I flipped over my bike. The bike landed on my head and into the pavement I went, causing scratch marks on my two front teeth. I got up, in shock, because I couldn't believe what just happened, and everybody had already ridden past me. I was alone with a head, tooth, and knee injuries, but I grabbed my bike and limped home. I didn't cry even though the pain was severe. The incidence was a learning experience. I am a true warrior. I can take a licking and keep on ticking. Growing up with my Dad made me tough.

When my grandmother was alive, I took her through many changes. I needed attention above and beyond the call of duty, and there was absolutely nothing I wouldn't do to get it. When the bond between a mother and daughter is broken, it is difficult to rationalize your wants, needs, and emotions. I just couldn't comprehend why my mother left me. So, by the age of eight years, I just grew more frustrated inwardly about my Mom and her whereabouts and her love for me. My Dad's family tried to make provision for what I lost. It wasn't enough and I began to rebel. I would do things, e.g. pass out on the floor, cut my hair, and write on the walls in the house. I would only do this when my Dad wasn't around. However, he would find out, of course, and I would get into big trouble.

I couldn't get away with much around my Dad, but I did get a little crafty with the hair-cutting situation. I told him that I had ringworms on my scalp from making mud pies outside with my best friend (we would make them with water; we had old school 80's fun), and that is why I cut my hair. He believed me until my grandmother pulled the hair that I had cut out from behind the radiator. I hid it there because it was the first place I could think of. I remember it as if it happened yesterday. My Dad came into the back room and said, "Lakisha I am going to ask you again what happened to your hair, and if you lie to me you will get a whipping."

I said, "Okay, I cut my hair," and I still got a whipping. He tricked me, or should I say, I tricked me for doing it. It took forever for my bangs to grow back. I was suffering on the inside and didn't know how to deal with my pain.

I sang in the choir during childhood and into my adolescent years. I tried to sing louder than everyone. I just felt the music deep in my soul. I didn't get my ear pulled, but I am sure the choir director wanted to. School and church plays were fascinating to me. I needed to be noticed, and the one successful way I could get attention was to make people laugh. Even today, I still like to make people laugh.

I still have the same craving for attention at times that I did as a child, but it has turned into advocacy for people who need help. I am an advocate for many causes these days. I have turned my need for my mother's love into something constructive. I perform at various events for Rape and Domestic Violence; I teach expressive dance; I write and read poetry, and I write skits. I have adopted a limelight personality. I am never afraid of the lights, camera, and action; it helps me to be creative and motivating! I learned to hold my head up high from my Dad's long-term girlfriend. She was a dark-skinned sister that was proud of her complexion and very confident in herself. I picked up on that trait and it changed my perception.

As time passed, I learned to cope with not having my mother around, even though I felt empty and confused. In my house, we never discussed my mother unless I mentioned her. My assumption is my Dad had to deal with his own emotions concerning her abandoning him too. During my mother's absence, I gravitated toward my friends' mothers looking for love, or any women who would give me their undivided attention.

The crazy thing about all of this is that I started to become rebellious and angry but not visibly so, it was all bottled up inside of me. Rebellion means to disobey one in control or authority. I would take my frustrations out on my Dad's family, but not the people at school or in my neighborhood. I was feisty with my cousins and aunt and passive in my neighborhood. I really had a lot of anger in me after my grandmother passed. I lost the two women that I held close to my heart within a five-year radius.

You know how the warm touch of a mother's love feels when you have felt it. You know what love is when you see it and feel it yourself.

I was shown love and felt the warm touch of my mother's love. Yet, she disappeared on me, out of sight and out of touch. To help ease the pain, I would sing a song that was close to my heart and touched my soul. The song means 'mother' in Swahili. At the age of five, I was overwhelmed when my mother disappeared. The pain that I felt made my heart ache. Yet, I still rolled with it, leaned with it, and rocked with it. I wear my pain as I wear my tattoos. My mother was gone, and I didn't see her again until seventeen years later.

If you have lost your mother, because of different causes, I understand your pain. Embrace your emotions and be prepared for a very slow healing process, at least it was, and still is, that way for me. *Your Deliverance is Coming!*

My Dad was a good father, but I longed for my mom. My Aunt Willie and her daughter, Tonya, were the only two remaining women in our family to reside in the house with me and my Dad. I really gave them attitude. I remember one day hurting Tonya's feelings when she asked for my hand as we were crossing the street. I said, "No, you are not my mother!" Eventually, I would pay for that comment. When I needed something from her, she would remind me that she wasn't my mother. However, later in life, she forgave me, and we reconciled our differences. I really needed my mother. I longed to crawl in her arms and tell her about all the things that were going on in my life that my Dad wouldn't understand, or so I thought. When I was younger, I would see women at the bus stop or the movies with their daughters and I would get angry and envious of their relationships. I just wanted to know why my life seemed bad, why did she leave me? What did I do to make her leave me? When I turned twenty-three, I read a book called, *'Damaged Emotions, Recovering from Memories, the Causes of Our Pain,'* by David A. Seamands. The book helped me realize that I was still sick in my soul after all these years. As I read, the following passage stood out: *"What are some of these damaged emotions? One of the most common is a deep sense of unworthiness, a continuous feeling of anxiety, inadequacy, and inferiority and inner nagging that says, 'I'm no good! I'll never amount to anything! No one could possibly love me. Everything I do is wrong."* Afterwards, I knew the Holy Spirit was talking to me. God was prompting me to look inwardly and acknowledge what was happening so He could heal me. As I continued reading, I read this statement, *"The good news of the Gospel has not penetrated down into the damaged inner scars, and those scars must be touched and healed by the Balm of Gilead."* Now I was sure that God had the right girl. He was talking to my sin-sick soul.

I purchased an inspirational CD on *healing* and further discovered the emotional destruction that I faced. What a wake-up call! The healing process continued. Through many tears, prayer and my investigative techniques, God brought my mother back to me after seventeen years. I found her when I was twenty-one. A coworker helped me find my mom. We conducted an internet search for her name in Buffalo N.Y.—that city and state remained in my memory. I know I am where I am today because God is on my side, and He promised never to leave me.

I was often told that I never would find her, but I am a dreamer. I dream real big. I have faith bigger than a mustard seed. However, when praying to God, I am learning to be more detailed. I asked for my mother's return, but I didn't ask God to heal my heart fully before I found her.

When I called her house, my sister answered the phone. She was born a few years after my brother and my Mom kept her. She was fourteen years old. After identifying myself, she said that our Mom told her about me. Our Mom was at work, so I left my home and work number for her to return the call.

Finally, my Mom and I reconnected, and she was shocked to hear my voice and know that her child found her after seventeen years. I was so happy to find her and she knew it. We arranged our first visit, which entailed a twelve-hour bus trip to Buffalo to see both her and my sister. When I arrived, we talked for hours. I told her stories about my life.

On my second visit, I shared some of the material I began writing for my new book, and our visit turned into a disaster. When she read portions that she didn't agree with, she got angry, shouting words about my Dad and how his nephew raped me. I defended my Dad by stressing that if she hadn't left me, the rape would have never occurred. She was furious and threw her phone at me. I remember looking at her and saying, "You are lucky you are my mother."

Her reply was, "I am still your mother, and you will not disrespect me. You've got to go." My bus was leaving in a few hours, so I left. Her friend drove me to the Greyhound station, destination Washington, D.C. I never imagined that my book would cause a conflict between us, but it did for a short while.

I had never treated her poorly. I just asked her why she didn't look for me. She told me that she was afraid I would reject her. I didn't like that answer, but it was her answer. I don't want to sound mean but, if I had been in her position, I would have just wanted to make sure that my baby was okay. I wouldn't have cared about the possible rejection. My quest for my mother's love landed me in more painful situations than I could have ever imagined. God had already written my life story a long time ago. Although there were detours, His plans for my life remain in effect.

I know what I'm doing. I have it all planned out—plans to take care of you, not abandon you, plans to give you the future you hope for.—Jer. 29:11

Life without my mother affected me to where I had an emotional breakdown in my group meeting at the D.C. Rape Crisis Center. It was Tuesday, on a cold rainy night in November. I told myself that I wasn't going to speak that night but, toward the end, I started to feel my soul crying out, so I began speaking. I expressed my heart to twelve women in my group.

I didn't understand why I yearned for my mother's love through other women and why I believed that any woman who told me they loved me would eventually abandon me like my mother did. I began crying while sharing a story about an older woman I worked with, trusted, and admired, had disappointed me. I was crying so badly that the entire group felt my pain, and some started to cry with me. I wanted the pain to go away. I get attached to older women, but keep my guard up because of previous betrayals. For clarity purposes, I repeated my statement. Insomuch as anyone in the group wanted to get close to me, they already knew where I stood. After the group meeting, I rode the train with one of the women. We continued our conversation. I remember stating, "I want my daddy." She insisted on taking me to the nursing home to see him. When we arrived visiting hours were over, but I didn't care. I wanted to give my daddy a hug and tell him that I loved him. My Dad always told me he loved me, and he showed me how much he cared. However, the kind of love that I needed was from a woman, it was a love he could never give me even if he tried.

Several women taught me how to conduct myself like a lady. Every woman who showed me how to be a woman was taught by the influences in their life.

I have different views on how to be a lady, some good and some bad. Nevertheless, they wanted to teach me; I guess for the sake of my Dad. People knew that he was a single Dad, and he was raising me by himself. Some knew us from the neighborhood or church. Many of my coworkers helped when I told them my story. I started working when I was just seventeen; at that age, I was still evolving into adulthood. Each woman taught me something different; some taught me about men and sex, while others taught me about hygiene, and how I should conduct myself as a young lady; some kept me grounded in the word of God.

There are four women in my life that I consider mother figures who truly love me: Tonya, my cousin; and Lynda, my godmother. Lynda became my godmother when I was eight years old. She saw my Dad and me at church and knew he needed help. Tonya is my cousin, my Dad's sister's daughter. She is ten years older than I am and has always been an old kind soul in my eyes. Unlike me, she had the opportunity to spend more time with our grandmother. Therefore, she would step in and help take care of me. She often took me to my doctor's appointments. When I was in elementary school, she encouraged me to read to her. She carried me everywhere with her. Being a type of a mother figure, I love her for her willingness to step in and help my Dad take care of me. There is much to be said about her, but it would consume most of this chapter. Later, you will read more about her.

My godmother Lynda showed me that if you put your mind and energy into success, you could be successful. She is a very successful hardworking woman. She once gave me a work assignment where I had to list all 50 states by writing them on the board. I couldn't wait until my Godfather, her husband, came downstairs in hopes he would save me. At the time, I didn't realize she was educating me. She wanted me to acquire some of her intellectual qualities. I am an official student of the school of my godmother Lynda. I love her for the quality time she spent to educate me. She and my Godfather spoiled me with their generosity. They bought me so many clothes and took me everywhere. My greatest adventure was visiting Disney World. Upon my father's approval, they became my godparents.

Renee, my best friend's mother developed a close relationship with me, as I got older. When Shaun went to college, I slept in her room. All the luxuries she had, I now had, along with their young daughter, whom I consider my baby sister, May. Renee took care of her household and me. There were so many serious issues in my life, and she never judged me by them. The stakes were high. I developed an emotional bond with her and couldn't let go. She received the most grief from me because I couldn't separate reality from my personal feelings. When I needed her, she was there. She held me accountable. My love for her runs deep. Nevertheless, deep inside, I still yearned for my mom.

Ms. Wonderful, my retired supervisor who embraced me as her daughter, her son and I birthday is January 24th, ten years apart, completes the four. I love them all, but I didn't come out of their womb. Therefore, I never felt complete and whole. I felt empty inside. In an attempt to make my life complete, the pressure I placed on these women was enormous as if they were my biological mothers. As I got older, I recognized my behavior and backed away from the relationships, a little bit.

THE DREAM

I had a dream in which I will not share with the world at this time but, just a few people know about it.

I revealed my dream to a woman I felt comfortable with. She was a nurturing mother who could identify with my feelings and give me Godly advice. I said, "I know this book is anointed and sometimes I can't touch it. I think my dream meant my past died and this book signifies my rebirth. I know God guided me to write about my life because He wanted people to know who He is and how He works. On many occasions, His spirit overshadowed me, which gave me strength to carry on. I hope the words conveyed herein would change lives from the inside out.

A couple of years ago, I visited a friend at church. A female minister was there praying for people. I approached the altar for prayer because I can always use that in my life. When my turn came, the minister instructed me to lift up my hands. She touched them and told me that God said to tell me do not stop writing. Keep writing. It was an overwhelming experience; she didn't know me, and she was a guest speaker that day. Thanks to her, I was inspired once more to continue writing. I knew I was on the right path. Remember, God is real and He loves you. Listen to the prayers of the sinner because He said that He would take the foolish and make them wiser than those who are reported as wiser.

I wanted my mother to embrace God, but I came to understand that she was just too ashamed to confront the truth. I often wondered how my sister felt about our reconnection. My mother and I stopped talking because I reminded her of the curse.

One year had passed. My Mom called to share some breaking news. She said, "Lakisha, your sister is pregnant." I cried like a baby, not just any old baby, but like a whiny baby. *The curse*, I thought to myself as I cried. My daughter wasn't in existence yet. With the little breath I had left, I managed to say, "Mom, the mother, and daughter relationships in this family are severed. It seems like we are under a curse.

I said a mouthful. My mother got so upset about the truth that she started arguing with me as if I said something wrong. She couldn't handle the truth of revelation that God showed me. God walks in Spirit and Truth, *regardless* of us and our own pride and shame.

I sat down and wrote this letter to her, after thinking about everything that we have expressed since I reunited with her.

First, I would like to apologize for yelling at you because you are my mother and I must respect you.

I want you to know that my book is not written to hurt anyone. I didn't want to write a book. This is something that God had put in my heart since 1999, before I even attempted to find you. I know that there are two sides to every story and my father told his side before I knew your whereabouts. Yes, you told me your side of the story regarding your relationship with my father, and it will be in the book.

You said there's a lot of hate in me, which is not true. When you read any book about a person's life, you would see that they will give a history of their family and their life, and then it will end on a good note. The scenario is similar to a book my sister is reading for one of her classes. If hate were in me, I would have displayed it when you hit me with your phone. "Hate has no mercy." So, if I were hateful, I would have shown you. Believe me when I say I have changed, and you don't really know me yet. God is a healer, and he can restore broken vessels. My heart is a vessel that pumps out so much love and pain. God has come in and started the process of separating the two, so they don't pump out both love and pain at the same time.

There are things in this book regarding my father's family that they don't agree with, but the truth is the truth. There are things that I have to expose about myself in this book. I don't want to, but this is God's project, so please talk to Him about this book. I would appreciate it if you do.

I truly believe that you are hurting and have not forgiven yourself for leaving your responsibilities behind. You say that you have given it to God, but discernment tells me otherwise. Every time I come up there, you act semi-antisocial, meaning you talk to me, but you keep me at a distance. I know that you are hurting because you didn't even try to find me.

You are my mother; you could have called Howard Hospital for my birth record to get my social security number or just to find out if I was still living. It was me who took the steps to find you, not your family, nobody, just me.

I believe that we will be able to get along if you stop comparing our relationship to the one between you and your mother. I am Lakisha Davis, and the way God is going to heal me is going to be different from the way He healed you.

Do you know what infirmities are? The Bible speaks of it. I have a wounded spirit and only God can heal me. You can talk to me until you are blue in the face, but God is the author and finisher of my life, and He knows what I am going through. You will never know until you humble yourself and ask Him.

Being apart for so many years, there was a serious disconnection. Now we are working towards rebuilding our connection. Although she's back in my life, a void remains in my heart. She has been gone for so long, I've adopted the phrase "out of sight, out of mind." Sometimes I forget to pick up the phone to call her. We both are a work in progress.

Now, my Mom and I talk and laugh together. When she cries, I am there to give her words of encouragement. She told me her strength is increasing and her faith is growing stronger. My mother is now saved and free from a life of misery and pain. She asked me in 2014 to please forgive her for not taking care of me. I expressed my forgiveness to her, and I meant it. Now, I understand the spiritual side of forgiveness. For my sanity, God delivered her from that demon, and we are rebuilding our relationship. God brought both of her children back to her, my brother and me. I made sure that when I turned eighteen years old I would find my brother and I did. He didn't know anything about our mother. Secrets in the family are astonishing. God is always good in the midst of it all. He is a restorer and a healer to those who are broken in spirit.

I was blessed with a daughter, and I know that I over compensate her. Serenity is spoiled rotten. I love her dearly, and I want her to understand her mother's love. A mother's love is very special. I put forth the effort to understand her feelings and the way she processes life at her age. Some days I feel as if I may be making a mistake by doing too much for her. But, I know that my insecurities are the driving force to ensure she lacks nothing. Yes. I am an enabler to her spoiled ways. For example, she has gone to at least three live concerts; she gets her nails and feet polished at the beauty parlor and goes to the hair salon regularly. Her room is decorated, and she has a closet full of everything, much more than I had when I was her age. We have our daily conversations while sitting at the table, no TV, or listening to the radio, just us. I always want to know what is going on in her little head. I give her work assignments like my Godmother gave me. She loves it. She is very smart.

Just as my Dad introduced me to God, I introduced her to God and taught her the power of prayer. I teach her to be respectful and use her manners at all times. I was taught as a child, when there's a thunderstorm God is talking, and to be still and listen. I suggested she did the same. My daughter has faith. Of all things on this Earth I want for her before I return to my Creator, I need to know that she has faith in God. When

I enter eternity, I want God to say to me, "Well done," when it comes to my guardianship over Serenity. I envision God holding me in his loving arms as I softly sing melodies in my heart to Him.

"Your Deliverance is Coming!"

CHAPTER 2

Getting Past the Mental Pain of Rape

It was a Friday night in 1984; I was five years old, and my Dad asked his niece to look after me overnight while he went to work. My cousin, Tonya, was around fifteen years old, and we went to our older cousin's, Jane and Jill's house, they had kids my age. My older cousins convinced Tonya to hang out with them by assuring her that Jason, their brother, would watch us kids. There were five children in the apartment, including me. We were all watching Friday night music videos, and once the videos went off, Jason said it was time for us to go to bed. I slept in a bed by myself. That night I wore a nightgown; once I fell asleep, I felt a breeze blowing up my leg. I remember pulling my nightgown down about three times, and then the unspeakable happened. Jason (who was an adult) jumped on my back, covered my mouth, and sodomized me. I was helpless. I was unable to do anything but scream, but nobody heard me because his grip muffled my screams. The pain inflicted upon me was indescribable. When he got off my little body, I had enough sense to run to the bathroom and lock the door before he returned for me. As the blood gushed from my body and down my legs, I fell on my knees and leaned over the bathtub, because I couldn't sit down. It was a real crime scene. As I waited for my cousins to come home, I cried uncontrollably. I was confused, scared, and in pain. I cried out to a God I never really knew, and from that day, I believe He has walked with me. As I waited for Tonya to return, I thought I heard the front door open. When I opened the bathroom door to peek out, I saw my cousin, Jason, with a knife in his hand. I shut the door again and locked it. They finally returned, and this time I heard their voices. Afterwards, all I remember was being in Children's Hospital with my Dad, getting two shots in my rear end and speaking with a child psychologist. She placed two doll babies on the table, one girl and one boy, and she asked me to show her what happened to me. I remember putting the boy doll baby on the back of the girl doll baby. At that point, I think my Dad lost a part of his mind. When my Dad and I left the hospital, we rode the bus home. I was the only person standing up. This woman looked at my Dad as if he was crazy because he was sitting down and I wasn't. She even offered her seat, but my Dad said, "No, she is okay." I can only imagine the pain my Dad felt on that long bus ride home. To this very day, I don't believe he has healed from the situation.

Jason went to prison for eight years for raping me, but he still wasn't free from his demons. The day he was released from prison, he came to my Dad's house and asked if he could rent a room. My Dad asked him if he were suicidal, and looked at him with rage in his eyes. My Dad was very hostile about the entire situation. He didn't take matters into his own hands because he worried about my well-being if he went to prison. That day, my best friend and I were leaving the neighborhood store, and I saw Jason from a short distance. I shared it with Shaun. After all those years, my spirit knew it was him. I was thirteen years old.

My Dad felt so bad about what had happened to me that he refused to talk about it ever again. He felt that he was protecting me from the painful memories. As a result, my Dad resorted to church ministry to bandage my wounds. He did what he knew best to help me, but professional therapy would have helped me too. Going to church helped me to overcome some of the most difficult mental scars of being raped.

I never knew that emotions had so many layers, like an onion. God alone had kept me sane during moments when I truly thought I was going to lose my mind. My hopes, dreams, and visions were fading fast. In my deepest moments of despair, I praise God, who intervened and gave me the strength to carry on. Thank you Jesus, my Lord, and Savior, for the gift of salvation, and saving my soul! I was lost but you found me. Glory Hallelujah! Reader, when I think about God's goodness and where He has brought me from, I must pause and give Him praise.

Being raped at a young age is no joke, it really affects how the brain functions. I am aware how my brain processes my thoughts and the way I interpret situations. For example, Serenity and I were walking to the store one day, close to a wooded area. From out of nowhere, a man walked behind us. Suddenly I stopped, turned around, looked at him, and said, "I am not an easy target." I said it with a militant tone and stern look on my face. I was not playing. I think about what happened to me when I was her age. Therefore, I am adamant about protecting my daughter and me. I will die fighting before anybody takes advantage of me again or even thinks about hurting my daughter. The man looked at me and smiled and said, "No, I was running for the bus, or something to that degree.

I am consciously aware of her safety especially when I am not with her; e.g., schools nowadays are not always safe. I am very cautious about her sleeping over other people's houses. Therefore, limitations were set in place. I don't put her in situations that I think are harmful, but you never know whom you can trust when you have experienced what I have. I have made it clear to men that I am sensitive and overprotective regarding my daughter's safety. When family betrays your trust, you just don't know what regular folk will do. The demons in Jason came back for me and this time they came to kill me because he had contracted AIDS in prison. If you don't believe in demons, but you believe in God and angels, then please study more about the spirit world because there are good and evil spirits out there, and he surely had some evil ones in him. I believe in human behavioral problems, but I also believe in demonic activity. He wasn't saved or baptized, so demons find people like him easy targets. I learned later on that he was saved during one of his hospital stays. Guess who prayed for his soul to be saved before he died? My cousin, Tonya, she asked him if he wanted to be saved, and he said yes. I know she did this because God led her to. Tonya is very spiritual. I haven't reached her level yet. When the news reached me, I remained silent. I didn't want to let on that I knew because I wasn't ready to speak on the subject. I was too emotional. I wanted him to go to hell, that is what my fleshy-self wanted, not my spiritual side.

Kids are abducted and sexually assaulted frequently. My first question is where are the parents? However, things can happen very quickly.

The inner torment I suffered from being attacked so violently left scars on my soul and mind. Those scars affected my motherhood. I find myself watching males closely when they are around my daughter. I will never let my guard down when it comes to protecting my child. I remember once Serenity was sitting on her daddy's lap; I politely walked over and placed her on his knee. He didn't say anything because he knew that I still battled with being sodomized. I know he wouldn't hurt her, but my deliverance was in progress.

In this season of my life, my trust in God has increased. I've made much progress by allowing Him to develop me. I don't know everything, and I can't foresee anything either; therefore, I decided to let God lead me. He is so good to me. He never failed me then, and I know He won't fail me now. I believe that I will be completely healed emotionally and mentally.

During the healing process, I attended group meetings at the D.C. Rape Crisis Center. My emotions were in turmoil, but everyone looked up to me because I was the only one in the group who had told on my predator at a young age; everybody else kept their abuse a secret until later on in life.

Families can be very secretive and are known to cover up the truth, especially on important issues such as family rape or anything else that brings negative attention to the family. I advise you to take the covers off the madness and free yourself from the chains of deception. Remember to pick your battles because not every battle is worth fighting. However, this fight called sexual abuse, especially when it involves kids, needs to be dealt with.

One day, while attending the group meeting, I wasn't 'Smiley, the Group Hero,' I was Lakisha, a hurt and confused child. I told my group, with tears streaming down my cheeks, that I found out where Jason lived, and I was feeling a bit threatened which caused a deep anger to rise in me! Everybody started crying, and the group counselor was concerned because they had never seen me in this condition.

Later, I discovered that Jason was dying of AIDS and had one month to live. The news was shocking, but I wanted revenge. It was too late; I found out that Jason, my abuser, died in the fall of 2005.

I asked his sister what happened to him, and she confirmed that he died of AIDS. My emotions didn't know which way to go, so I reverted within all day. My cousin, Tonya, who lived with me, kept in contact with his side of the family. I thought she should have mentioned it to me, but she didn't. Later that week, I went home and asked my cousin why she hadn't told me about Jason. Her response was, she didn't want to tell me because she knew I would have a bad reaction. This was an assumption on her part. Finding out from someone else caused a bad reaction; I was upset.

When I told my father about Jason's death, he reacted just as I had expected. He showed no remorse. I guess he believed the big payback had come and justice was served. My father expressed, "Had it not been for the fact that he needed to be around to take care of me, he would have been in the penitentiary due to his hostile attitude toward the rape."

I learned a lot trying to get beyond the mental pain of rape. Jason was full of the demons that took control of him. I had my cousin's kids with me one weekend. She and her children are Jason's nieces. I asked her girls if Jason ever touched them. They said no. The eldest of the two also said that, on the day he died, she was there when he came in the house. As he prepared to take his medicine, breathing became difficult. His niece asked if she should call 911, and she did. The paramedics operated on him, but it didn't help. The niece responded by saying, "He doesn't have a heart anymore, and he can't remember us." I was numb. After I had found out he was cremated, I asked a cousin who lived with Jason's sister if I could see his ashes. I couldn't believe that I wanted to see his ashes, but I did. Since it was just us in the apartment, she granted my request.

My cousin brought a green box to the dining room table with Jason's ashes in them. I removed the top from the box and saw a plastic bag with a zip tie on it. I pulled it out the box and light dust of ashes came out. At that very moment, I felt anger, rage, and happiness all at once. The look on my face was spooky, I am sure, because my cousin looked at me as if I was crazy and, for a moment, I was. Upon returning the bag to the container, I noticed his crushed up bones in the ashes too. I said aloud, "You hurt me, and now I am holding your bones and ashes." I felt that uttering those words would bring me closure, and it did for a moment because I sense that his demons still haunt me.

I had a dream about Jason, which made me realize that I am still trying to break free of the pain he inflicted on me. In the dream, I was in my old house, and Jason was chasing me. I was running for dear life. Then, I just stopped dead in my tracks, turned around, and said, "Why did you rape me?" I wanted to know because I needed closure as to why my heart, mind, body, and soul were hurting so bad that I couldn't move on. I needed to know for my own sanity. He just looked at me and smiled. It was a wicked smile, and I woke up very angry.

There were stories circulating about his life, so I investigated further because they were puzzling. I need to be free from the spirit of pain in this area of my life. There were others who played a major role in his wicked affairs by allowing him to harm innocent children through their awareness of his actions, but doing nothing to stop it. I was a visitor at their house that dreadful night. I can't help but wonder what happened to the kids who lived there.

Coincidentally, as I was in route to see my father, I ran into Jason's sister, Jill, at Howard University Hospital at the age of thirty-four. I almost didn't recognize her, but she responded when I called her name. My first thought was to ask her why she allowed her brother to hurt me. I bit my tongue, literally, but I told myself that if I saw her again, I would bring up the topic about her brother raping me. Lo, and behold, the next day I saw her and knew it was meant to be. My Dad was in the hospital, and asked me to check on Jill's mother, who was in the hospital, when I entered the room she was sitting there. She was shocked to see me because I never really knew their mother or had a relationship with her. She was my grandfather's daughter from his previous marriage, before he married my grandmother.

She asked me how I was doing and if I had heard from my mother. I told her yes, but our relationship was a bit strained, due to guilt she dealt with for leaving me. My cousin began giving me advice about my mother. I laughed on the inside. I said to myself, 'You got some nerve trying to give me advice.' Therefore, I said, "You know I am writing a book about my life?" I told her about Chapter 1, life without my mother, and then I told her about Chapter 2, getting past the mental pain of rape. Her eyes widened and the first words she said were, "I felt so bad about what Jason did to you." She told me when they arrived home that night in 1984; they saw me bleeding, and she smacked him in his face and he walked out the door. Afterward, she ran some bath water and put me in the tub while Tonya called the police. CPS called my Dad to tell him what happened to me because Tonya and Jill were too scared to tell him.

The conversation got very personal. She told me that her brother had many demons and that he was sick. He was sexually abused in foster care, after being placed there due to family issues. She stated that Jason

25

abused others. While she lived a street life and had to deal with her own personal challenges, she believed she had no control over what she allowed to happen. For years, I was angry with her, but doing our conversation, I felt healing and deliverance taking place inside me.

In the Bible, there is a story about a woman at the well (John 4th chapter) who was approached by Jesus. She didn't expect to be healed, but she was. Nonetheless, she met a man who talked to her about her life and gave her insight as to why she did the things she did. Jesus healed her from sexual impurities. Now, if the woman at the well just happened to be healed, then I know my desire to be touched by the Healer is not far away. Why? I truly believe in healing and the power behind it. Yes! I am just a human. I had never visited the places the Bible speaks of nor have I walked the streets that Jesus walked when He went to heal people and lands from illness, but I truly and honestly believe it. The Bible says that if I knock, the door shall be opened, and if I seek healing, I will find it (Luke 11:9). This is where my faith comes in despite my double-mindedness at times. There are moments when I take fate into my own hands and try to heal my mental scars by myself. I have the gift of healing/therapist in my own way, but I await the healing touch of the Master Physician Himself.

I have a Black art painting that I bought from an art show. In this painting, it shows a woman washing Jesus' feet with her hair and tears. It is a side view of Jesus' face. In reality, we don't know how he looked, but the Bible describes Him as having bronze skin and hair like wool (Daniel 7:9-10). The painting is hanging on the wall in my living room. It reminds me that God can heal me despite all the suffering I endured as a result of being raped as a child. I use to sit in my living room, light candles, and stare at the painting, hoping and praying that one day I too will be touched and made whole again.

The story of the woman in the painting is a Biblical story, and this is the interpretation. She was a prostitute who saw Jesus. Feeling ashamed, she fell at his feet and asked for mercy. Her heart was broken because she had committed so many sins in her body and wanted to be free. Jesus already knew her story, but Peter, one of his disciples, was silently thinking to himself, "If Jesus knew who this female was he wouldn't want her to touch him at all." Jesus heard his thoughts, but Peter didn't know that until Jesus asked Peter a trivial question. He said, "Peter, if two men owed me money and one of them had a higher debt than the other, which one do you think I would pardon?" Peter replied, "The person with the lower debt." Wrong answer. Jesus told Peter that he would pardon the person who had the higher debt, because He is merciful (Luke 7:41-50). I am thankful for that story. I have always felt there is nothing I could do that was so bad that I couldn't be pardoned. I knew that God was going to heal me because I stood firm in my faith. I was never a prostitute, but I indulged in pre-marital sex. I can relate to the shame and brokenness inside and desperately wanting to get to Jesus. No matter what others say about me, I continue to reach for Him.

I saw a movie that triggered many issues within me. One main trigger was being raped by my cousin at an early age and not forgiving him for the pain he caused me. In the past, I indirectly distributed pain to those I was intimate with. My ability to love wholeheartedly was slim, even though I yearned for love. Today, I am receiving the type of love that I so longed for from my husband.

Based on my perception of men, I never thought that I would ever be in a serious relationship with a man because of the games they played with me. I decided to remain single until Serenity turned fourteen. At that age, she would be old enough to defend herself if my date made the wrong turn in her bedroom; that is how my mind functioned. Therefore, when God sent King David, my husband, into my life it startled me. In the beginning of our relationship, I questioned whether God sent him.

To escalate matters, I conversed with my Aunt Precious about David. She told me not to let my insecurities dictate my future. She said if that man loves you let him love you. Don't end up old and alone. She said, "Don't pass up the love that is presenting itself to you." My response was, "my heart is guarded; it is heavy with all kinds of hurts." I also told her that my pain is so familiar to me it is hard to let love in. She told me to let it go and release it to God. In her wisdom I found some peace. My Aunt Precious was an angel who helped to guide me. I could talk to her about anything. I needed her to help me make sense of it all. My Aunt Precious passed away a few weeks later. She will forever live in my heart because her wisdom lives in the new life given me. Our spirit never dies just our bodies. I believe we will live forever, as our souls do not die. Thank you Aunt Precious, I love you!

The test of true love was in effect. When the rain and storms of life came, David weathered them with me like the true solider he is. If he could survive the Iraq war, then certainly he could handle me. After witnessing his actions, he broke down my Great Wall of China, as he called it. For years, sexual intimacy was distorting to me. True affection and real intimacy were something I didn't understand until I was married. God sent him to love me despite my flaws.

My husband believes that I can't fully love him until I allow the Lord to continue the healing process. He believes the Lord will heal me because of his faith and mine. I believe that too. My husband reassured me he wouldn't ever leave me, and in marriage, if the Lord takes me away first, he will die shortly thereafter from heartbreak. I can see the seriousness in his eyes when I tell him to *live* on and keep my memory alive. He didn't make any promises, but he said I am his other rib.

I shared with my husband the sorrow I sometimes feel for him, because he started courting me in a season when I was undone. I didn't seek therapy for twenty years and never totally healed from the trauma. My husband is aware of my insecurities based on my actions. He told me that God Almighty would not bring a man like him into my life to hurt my child or me in any way. He understands that movies and certain things trigger me, bit he reassures me that everything will be alright and inspires me to continue to listen, pray, and trust God.

Serenity's grandmother on her Dad side worked at a nursing home. I dropped her off once, but I went in this time. After greeting another lady who lived in the nursing home, and had a condition in which she was bent over, she grabbed me by the hand, pulled me down to her eye level and told me "NOBODY WILL EVER HURT YOU AGAIN!" My heart dropped! All I could say was Jesus Christ of Nazareth.

Reader, God is everything, and He loves you. If you have experienced sexual abuse, don't think that you are a bad person due to the unstable emotions you feel, as the pain grows deeper. In the aftermath, sometimes I would beat myself up about my emotions surrounding the rape. I grew up in church with a mindset to serve God. I was a choir member, and I attended every youth Bible Study and retreat that we had in my church. I even vowed to stay pure until I got married.

Unfortunately, I did not keep my end of the bargain. I couldn't deal with rejection at sixteen years old, so I gave my innocence to my first boyfriend Joseph. At sixteen, I discovered the power of what sex could do to you. When I was a little girl, the demons took what they wanted by force, through rape. As I grew older, lust and anger entered me. I grew up with feelings that I could not understand, sex practically came knocking on my door, and I willingly answered.

I knew the right thing to do, but I was still doing the wrong things. The spirit of confusion was challenging me. Sex became my stronghold, and I didn't have a clue why; it really didn't dawn on me until I turned twenty-four. I endured much heartache and pain due to pre-marital sex. I grew up knowing God, but I didn't know about demonic attacks until my mid-twenties. I learned how Satan will study you and continue to study you until he knows what to do to get you off the course that God designed for you. Temptation was presented to me in many forms, and I would just take what Satan offered, just as Eve in the Garden of Eden.

As I grew into womanhood, I recognized that I tried to fill a void within my soul when I would give my body to my boyfriends. I felt a little erratic sometimes but knew I had to release the anger raging inside of me in some way, good or bad. I believe there were evil forces influencing those negative thoughts.

The day was October 1, 2012. I was on my lunch break, and I decided to sit on the second floor by the big window facing the hotdog stand. Everybody loves the view and fortunately the table was available that day. I put my book and water bottle on the table to hold my spot so that I could go into the cafeteria and grab some chicken wings. When I returned, I saw Vision, one of my colleagues in the building, sitting there. She said to me, "Girl I didn't know this was your stuff. I was just going to ask whoever came to the table if they wouldn't mind if I join them."

I replied, "No problem." However, at that moment, I didn't recognize it was a divine appointment set up by God who wanted both of us to be there at that table together that day. We began talking about life and relationships, and I revealed to Vision that I was writing a book about my life. I named the first two chapters, and chapter 2 stood out to Vision. She was shocked to hear that I had been raped. I told her that I felt like a sacrifice for those who have been down this horrific alley and that my book was not only to tell my story, but to help those who are still hiding their abuse story. There are people in their forties and fifties who have been raped, and nobody knows about it, not even their family.

Vision started crying. She said, "I am one of those women." I was in shock that she had revealed this to me. Nobody else knew about this but her, her abusers, who were her own family members, and me. She told me that three different people in her family sexually abused her from the age of nine until she was twelve. I was blown away, especially when she told me that she interacted with them at family functions, and they act as if they never touched her, so she plays along with the deception. Vision always blamed herself for what happened. She is also fearful of exposing them; she has held on to this secret for all of these years. "Touch her Lord!"

I told her, "Satan has been lying to you Vision. He is the father of lies; there is no truth in him. He has planted lies in your mind regarding the sexual abuse to keep you in bondage." The tears began flowing down her face; my heart began to melt within me. The pain I felt emanating from her was so intense that tears began to flow down my face too. I pulled myself together because I felt that I needed to be her strength at that moment. God was using me to open the door to her road of recovery.

I explained to her the effects of child sexual abuse, and the behavioral issues that often follow when the issue has not been properly dealt with. She agreed to everything I said as truth because she could relate to the erratic behavior, amongst other things.

For those who have been abused, I suggest getting involved in a rape crisis group where others in the same situation come together and release the pain, so the healing process can begin. The road to recovery is bumpy, but you will make it through. As an act of faith, after removing the bandages from those wounds, each day start breathing life into the dead sore.

On January 28, 2007, four days after my 28th birthday, God used me to intervene in a family ordeal in which I didn't know the family. I was 8 months pregnant with Serenity. I went to a young woman's apartment to get my hair braided and overheard a conversation regarding a little girl and her sisters who lived on the bottom level in the apartment complex. I didn't know the lady disclosing the information, but it was stated that the girls complained that their vagina was hurting. The oldest who was five years old mentioned to the young lady that her Dad touches her on the weekends! As I processed the information, a man entered the apartment during the discussion and said he believed the statements were true.

I heard enough! I asked the young woman to bring the little girls upstairs so I could speak with them. I needed to know for myself what was going on. I refused to sit back, listen, and not take action if these allegations were true. When the five year old arrived, I took her in the back room and told her my name. I also gave her some candy while explaining to her that I too was once five years old and now I am a big girl just like she will be one day. She smiled. I asked her if anybody touches her in her private area; I showed her where her private area was by using a teddy bear. At first, she started biting her nails then backed away from me while having this fearful look in her eyes. I told her if she tells me I would not tell anyone. She said, "YES!" I pointed to my lips and asked, "Does anyone put their lips on you?" She said, "NO!" I asked, "Did someone put their private part on your private part? She said, "NO, just their fingers." I said, "So someone sticks their fingers in you?" She said, "YES!" I asked her if it hurts. She said, "YES!" I then asked her to tell me who the person was, and she backed away from me again biting her nails. I grabbed a teddy bear and asked her to show me what this person does to her, and she stuck her fingers out and pointed to the private part on the bear. I never disclosed to her that I was touched at her age because I wanted her to reveal to me exactly what happened.

I asked her again "Who is this person?" She said, "my Dad!" I gave her some bracelets I wore on my arm and asked her to remember me by them. I told her I would keep her and her sister safe.

None of the neighbors wanted to get involved. Therefore, I had to take fast action. I left the building and called Child Protective Services.

More facts became known concerning the things their father did to them, which are too graphic for this book. God used me to help those little girls, it was a long process, but I stayed the course. I went to court on their behalf. With my assistance, the girls were removed from the home of their abuser. In the end, they were placed with a wonderful woman whom I call Ms. Blessing. She lived in a beautiful home and had a wonderful family. Serenity and I spent Thanksgiving at her house. I cried like a baby when Ms. Blessing prayed over the food. My soul cried out Thank you JESUS! God is so good!

I don't mind other people's business, but when it comes to a child being harmed, it becomes my business. The passion in my heart for the innocent will not allow me to sit back knowing that a child, as I once was, is in danger, and I do nothing.

I have been on my road to recovery for more than five years now. The bandage came off unexpectedly. I was living my life, doing my thing, until one day God said, "It is time to deal with the issue." God knew the root to my behavior at times even when I didn't. I have to fight my emotions often to keep my head above water. Therapy, the group sessions, writing, dancing, and the spoken word were all tools I used to maintain and control my rage and pain. Let's not forget laughter, which is vital to me.

Of course, God has truly been the source of my strength. I have never seen God, but I know He is real; I know He is a healer, for a fact. If God could heal my cousin who had leukemia, I know He can heal others. My cousin has not had a drop of cancer in her body for many years now. Her medicine cost around one thousand dollars, but God healed her, and He did it for His glory and honor. He really wants people to know that He is God and all things are possible through Him.

When my emotions are triggered, I write. I wrote this poem at my desk one day at work, almost ten years ago. The inspiration to write came over me, so I started writing. This is how I felt about Jason and everybody else who hurt me.

Pieces of Me

Pieces of me have been scattered amongst the wolves,

Tearing at me for they're feeding.

As I sit back and watch how they enjoy my flesh, I begin to faint.

I am losing strength, I am losing blood, and I am losing my vision.

All the pieces of me have been torn to almost nothing.

The wolves came to eat my flesh because they knew of the spirit that resides in me.

The same spirit that hung on the Crucifix is the same spirit that lives in me.

They were able to smell the glory inside of me, so they wanted to destroy me.

But in the midst of their torture a loud voice from heaven said, "Peace Be Still."

At that moment, all demonic attacks stopped, and the wolves hastened to that voice.

With blood dripping from what was left, not torn off my body.

The Lord said, "Get Up!"

I paused and listened again, and He said, "Get up, Lakisha."

Miraculously, my limbs began to heal themselves and blood started to fill up in my body, within seconds my strength was back, and I was healed in the Name of Jesus.

Then the wolves started to turn on each other until there was not one wolf standing.

My pain, I have worn it like a tattoo but, in this year, I will no longer be a victim to the wolves that want to destroy me.

"Your Deliverance Is Coming" Jesus Is Lord.

"Smiley"

When Ms. Wonderful retired, she was replaced with this guy named Simpson. He was a young man who was very sociable, and he seemed nice. After a few months, he got married, and I went to his wedding. I thought he was a cool guy, but that all changed very quickly. It was the day of my evaluation; we met to discuss my performance. He said, "Lakisha, your friends aren't your friends because they talk about you behind your back and have told me some things about you; be careful whom you call your friends." I was in shock to hear this; he had only been in the office for six months and points this out to me. The stern side in me asked, "What does this have to do with my evaluation?" He replied that he was just looking out for me. I was pissed off. I think what I don't know doesn't hurt me, and now I am hurt. I told him to get the person who had been gossiping so the three of us could have a conversation. I was young and emotional, so I got up from my seat and said, "No, I will not be a part of this." I asked, "Where is your integrity? That comment angered him. Guess what his response was to me? "Lakisha, if you fight against management you will not win." That comment sent me down a dark path. My emotions caused me to feel defenseless like I felt when I was raped. I felt threatened, and I don't handle threats too well, especially from men. Simpson had to cover himself because he didn't want to be involved in the drama that he ignited. Her name was Scarlet; she was his boss and did everything to protect him. She really made it hard for me. I shed many tears in that office.

During that time, my Dad had health issues. I was there for him as usual. My work situation exacerbated. Prior to the drama incident, they were very understanding of the situation with my Dad. I was harassed by them both. I went to therapy because my PTSD was triggered. The environment was hostile. I didn't feel safe. I felt as if I was being taken advantage of.

My behavior was bizarre and erratic. One day I was at my desk and Simpson came into the office speaking loud saying, "It's hot in here; it's hot in here." Scarlet came out from her office to my desk and, without warning, said, "Lakisha, as of today no more heaters." Be mindful everybody in the office had a heater, but she told me I couldn't have mine.

I took a deep breath, and I kicked the heater so hard that one of the analysts ran to the front of the office because she thought a bomb had gone off. Once I kicked the heater, I snatched it out of the wall and handed it to her. Scarlet had an astonishing look on her face; I was ready for anything at that moment. I looked at her with the same rage.

I went to the proper authorities to discuss the matter and let them know that the environment was becoming too hostile for me. I was responding out of pain they were causing me.

I wrote this letter to Simpson in 2004.

How do I feel about you? I think that you are a good individual, but you prey on the weak, or those who appear to be weak in your eyes. I don't like you because of that, and I never knew that you were like that from getting to know you the first couple of months that you started working here. I believe that you were trying to be manipulative when you told me that my friends weren't my friends and that people talk about me behind my back. I believe that you also talked about me but covered it up with them just in case I was told something that made you look bad as my team leader.

You hurt me very badly because I did have respect for you, but you decided to use my life as your target practice throwing evil out of your mouth about me. So, therefore, stay the hell away from me. Don't say anything to me except good morning and good night. You are a man trapped in a child's mindset. You don't respect your own integrity or me.

In my eyes, you want to take my livelihood, my job from me. You are dangerous.

When I first met you, I looked into your eyes and saw that God was going to allow you to go through something to bring you closer to Him, and I told you that. I didn't know it was going to be because of me, and I didn't know that God was going to make you my enemy to draw me closer to Him too. You felt that if I didn't want to go along with the program in here, then I could just be fired, and that would be the better way out in your eyes. In my case, I wanted you to take management courses along with sensitivity classes.

It is freedom time for me. You, nor anyone else, will continue to hold me in bondage because I am a beautiful individual inside and out. I refuse to lay down while you walk all over me. I refuse to give up. I was born to fight for what I believe in, and I will not allow you to destroy me, "Do you hear me?"

One more thing, I am a woman, and you are a man; why are you using your God given authority to hurt and manipulate me? My Heavenly Father has heard my cry for help and He will see to it that I am protected from your evil snares.

Peace,

Lakisha N. Davis

My therapist released me from work for one week so I could get my mind together. A man, who caused my rape issues to resurface, was harassing me, and Scarlet was playing a part by approving of the foolishness.

Later, I was informed of a job opening in another office and was told to apply; I did and went on an interview. I was hopeful with anticipation of working in a different environment. The night after the interview, "God" spoke to me. He said if I forgave Simpson and Scarlet, then I would get this new job.

I couldn't believe my ears. I thought I was dreaming, but I wasn't; that was God's message to me. I prayed and cried because I felt so hurt that Simpson and Scarlet tried to ruin my reputation by their supposedly secret chats about me to others in the building. I forgave them because it was the right thing to do. I received a call from Inez, the Director in the new office to tell me I got the job! The weird part about all of this is that before all of this drama started, I had a dream that someone in the agency was trying to get me fired, and this woman came out of nowhere and stopped it from happening, she rescued me. I now know that the woman was Inez. Bless her heart.

I want to share with you information concerning Post Traumatic Stress Disorder. I researched the topic and prepared a report for a psychology class while attending the P.G. Community College. It's no surprise I studied to become a child psychologist, one day I will be.

Below are the definitions of Post-Traumatic Stress Disorder (PTSD)

- Women who were sexually abused at earlier ages are more likely to develop complex PTSD and borderline personality disorders.

- PTSD is an emotional illness that develops as a result of a terribly frightening, life-threatening, or otherwise highly unsafe experience.
- Chronic physical signs of hyper-arousal, including sleep problems, trouble concentrating, irritability, poor concentration, blackouts, or difficulty remembering things, increased tendency and reaction to being startled and hyper-vigilance to threat.
- Explosive anger, or passive aggressive behavior.
- Persistent feelings of helplessness, shame, guilt, or being completely different from other's; feeling the perpetrator of trauma is all-powerful and preoccupation with either revenge against or allegiance with the perpetrator.
- Anxiety, depression, and drug abuse are symptoms of PTSD.

Motta, Robert W. (2013). *Understanding and Treating Posttraumatic Stress Disorder.* Pennsylvania: Mental Health News, 15 (*1*).

You may not experience them all, but you will experience one out of the six. So get help today.

"Your Deliverance Is Coming!"

CHAPTER 3

Overcoming Insecurities

My insecurities were great which affected many areas of my life. I was insecure about myself, which provoked thoughts concerning my purpose in life. My personality is made up of so many elements. Moments when I felt unsure, my life seemed to spin like a whirlwind. My emotions were scattered in places that were out of my comfort zone. I felt insecure in male relationships. In retrospect, I came to the realization that I didn't know my self-worth. Had I known, I would not have allowed myself to stay in unhealthy relationships. Unproductive relationships slowed down my productivity because I was unequally yoked with men who weren't driven as much as I was about life.

They were good to me on a worldly level. They fed my flesh and gave me things, but the spiritual and ambitious elements were missing. As I observed myself closer, I clearly saw repeated behavioral patterns. A rumor reached my boyfriend implying, "Kisha falls for every dude she deals with." I confronted the situation. Although I was hurt by the rumor, it was a true statement. I did fall prey to wolves in sheep's clothes on occasion and felt that I loved them. I was around twenty-two years old at the time.

The truth pierced my heart and blew me away. I was hurt that my girl, my homie, would betray me, so I had no other choice but to distance myself from her. Eventually I forgave her. The truth caused me to change my swag in relationships. It was a pleasure meeting those men, because I learned a valuable lesson. I would be attached to a guy, and when the relationship ended, I would hold on for dear life to the dysfunction. I thought it was normal behavior for a woman to tolerate cheating. As long as I was labeled the "One," and benefiting in the relationship in some way, I stayed.

My competitive nature went after someone I felt I gave away. My relationship timing was off. The attachment to my lovers filled a void. After each breakup, the void within my heart intensified. If I could show you the pain that was lying dormant inside of me, it would bring you to tears; it was deeper than the ocean. I cried out to God to fill the void. I asked Him to do something great within me.

When I felt lonely, I wanted to call one of my lover's for affection. I would cry out to Jesus for comfort and compassion. I got tired of being hurt repeatedly and not understanding the root of my problems. "Bing," God gave it to me in a flash. He revealed to me that I was insecure.

While visiting my great-aunt, she explained insecurity to me. She said, "We attract people like ourselves, people who are looking for mothers and fathers in others, which in the end, causes severe pain. Then we walk around as if everything is okay, but we are hurting." She said God showed her an image of a sore sitting on her leg, and it wasn't healed, the sore symbolizes unforgiveness that we carry within ourselves when people hurt us. So, basically, we act as if we are okay in an unhealthy relationship, we say we forgive, but we really don't. It takes a long time for the wound to heal, but we manage to hide it when interacting with others.

My insecurities also caused my body to go through changes. I would lose or gain weight, depending on the situation. By allowing my insecurities to run my life, it robbed me of my peace.

For example, in 1998, I met a man at a cabaret. I was nineteen years old. He saw me; I saw him, and, because I am a woman, I turned away. Do you think I would show him that I was attracted to him? You know how men act when they are blessed and highly favored. Therefore, once the cabaret was over, he managed to find me to give me his number. I figured that since he sought me out, he was worth calling. I called him a couple of days later and we talked. This continued for a few days. At that point, I felt our conversations went well, so I invited him over. We went to a carryout located in Maryland. I sat on top of his '86 gray caprice and ate a fried chicken breast dinner with fries. I have always been a free-spirited person. I sat on his hood and ate while watching the stars. After I had eaten, we went back to my place to watch TV. We laughed and talked all night; I really enjoyed his company. Days went by and our conversations were stimulating. One day I lost control and my desires needed to be fulfilled. I wanted him close to me in an intimate way, but I wasn't his girl, but gave in to my desires anyway. This is when the twist began. I became attached and emotionally tied to this man. He was about eight years older than I was, so I am sure he was able to see signs of insecurity.

Here comes the separation. He called me from Florida in the summer of 1998. "What's up?" he asked. I smiled because I was happy to hear his voice, knowing he was out of town with his family, his whole family, including his baby's mother. He said that his family always includes her and the kids whenever they vacationed at his mother's timeshare. I felt special because he took the time to call me. As I reflect, I am so happy my deliverance came in this area. I told my friend that I wanted to get him something for his birthday because he showed me that he was considerate by taking the time to call me. Let's fast forward.

I established a relationship with his mother, Ms. Diamond. She told me she raised Terrance to believe in Christ. I could see after all these years he did have a strong foundation. His conversations were thought provoking. I couldn't believe that he was so in tune to the spiritual world.

I believe God answers prayers and that no one who has ever sought out God wasn't heard. The prayer that I wrote was answered. I didn't pray to God about breaking this unhealthy soul tie until I had enough of the dysfunction. In addition, he began to grow in his walk with God but he wasn't an angel. He just started understanding the spiritual world a little more than he did before. Our conversations became a little spiritual and rose to another level. However, the lust between us was still there.

One night, I had a dream that he and I were on motorcycles on the highway and we were racing. All of a sudden, I couldn't slow down; something was wrong with my brakes and people were getting hurt and even dying trying to get out of my way. Terrance couldn't do anything to help because I had already passed him. Once I reached Route 450 and saw the Capital Plaza sign, the motorcycle stopped, and Terrance was right beside me. I woke up in shock.

I asked God what He was trying to tell me. I believe He was telling me to slow down in my walk with Him because I had a lot of zeal but not enough knowledge and if I didn't people would get hurt by my actions. People are watching me. I see me in Christ, but it is not what I display all the time. I need to walk slowly in my spiritual path by paying closer attention and listening more than I talk. He also said, "even though Terrance wasn't where I was spiritually, he would catch up with me at a moderate pace; there was no need to speed through this process called life." God will have me where He wants me in due time. He wanted me to slow down. I am still in the slow process; my deliverance is coming.

It was now 2004, and I wanted out. I was still tied to this young man through other relationships in my life. I wrote on February 3, 2004, *"Thank you Lord for another day. Lord, help me not to expect anything more from Terrance. I can't even ask for too much more because he does not have the character traits that I am looking for, so help me to understand that. Lord, I love you and thank you again for being there for me even when I can't see you or feel you, but I know you are real. Please forgive me for my sins, and I thank you again. In Jesus Name, Amen."*

I had another dream that still haunts me. In the dream, I was running from a man with a knife in his hand; it actually looked like my first boyfriend, and I saw a church with two deacons standing outside. I ran to them and told them that someone was trying to kill me. The deacon to the left of me with the Bible in his hand said, "You are a child of God and Satan is trying to kill you, you have something special in you. I will take you home." I was so relieved and happy because I felt safe. As we started walking to his car, he grabbed me by my hand and pulled out the biggest knife I have ever seen in my life and said, "I've got you now." I woke up on my feet, and I ran out of that dream. I went into my kitchen with my Bible and asked God to talk to me, and I opened the Bible to, *2 Timothy Chapter 3*, where it states "in the last days, the children of God will almost be deceived by all kinds of spirits and weak-willed women will allow men and deception into their homes." Guess what? About ten minutes later, Terrance called me and said he was on the highway and the hood of his car had flown open. God was telling me to move on from Terrance. He was also telling me that I shouldn't believe or embrace everybody who talks about God or, because a person may tote a Bible or know the Word, it doesn't mean they are from God. Satan knew the Bible, too. Terrance wasn't the devil, but he was used by the devil to play on my insecurities. I would get close to people who talked about God, but their actions showed a different story. Some people are malicious and evil, but they profess they love God. I remain watchful. Granted nobody is perfect, not even me, the church girl from Fifth Street. Please! I have good intentions, but my downfall was self-pleasure when men invaded my space. As time went on, and I got older and wiser, I would not be so quick to allow myself to get too attached to men. I finally let go of Terrance.

Insecurities show up in various relationships. They show up in work relationships. Been there done that! Those who get joy out of making fun of a person's insecurities are horrible to me. Consciously, I have to make the decision to take the high road in this type of scenario, if I don't, anger will set in. People have been messing with me since I was five years old. Deliverance needs to take place before I enter Eternity, all I can do is smile. People do take my kindness for weakness, and sometimes I have to show people that I am not weak, but strong, not just physically but mentally.

Insecurities are a monster because you don't feel secure within yourself, which causes an irritating feeling inside. I know it is an evil spirit whose mission is to break me, but I refuse to be broken. Some things I am no longer insecure about, I refuse to be. How did I overcome some and not others? I used a high level of faith in that area. Don't ask me why I can't overcome them all. Some are like thorns in my side, and it keeps me humble. God made us so that we would be a reflection of Him in many ways, and I see some growth in me. I pray for myself and other people pray for me. Some don't believe that prayer works, but it does, especially when you have faith. I am like a child when it comes to wanting something from God, depending on what it is; I will remind Him that He said if I ask for anything in His name that He will give it to me, this includes allowing me to overcome insecurities. I don't beg God for external things, only internal things, like healing my heart and my mind from so much confusion and pain that dwells within me.

As I battled with insecurity, I began reading empowerment books and scriptures, which helped me to feel secure. I questioned God about my purpose and why I was put on this Earth. He answered! Everybody has something they don't like about themselves, so why should I feel slighted.

This body that I dwell in will one day be buried in the ground and my spirit will go back with God. In the light of this truth, I made some changes. My insecurities were a thing of the past and never returned in Jesus name! I read a book by Joyce Meyer called, *Ashes for Beauty*. What captured my attention was the part about security. When you are secure about yourself, you can be in a room full of all types of people, and you will stand out in a crowd when you exude confidence. Therefore, I began practicing confidence by walking with my head held high. When I spoke with people, I gave them direct eye contact. I tested myself to see if I still cared about what people would or would not say about me. If I walked past a group of women and they started laughing, I had to ask myself, "How do you know that they are talking about you?" You don't know, so I stopped assuming.

Growing up in an era when kids liked to joke around also played on my mental psyche. Being dark-skinned and thickly built was the first thing kids would notice about me and start to pick on me; these were boys.

I was being set up by society not to like me. The images shown on TV and the comments men would make concerning what constitutes beauty, confused my self-perception.

I remember when I wouldn't smile openly; I would cover my mouth or smile without showing my teeth. I remember wanting to bleach my skin, because I thought lighter was better. I was a twelve year old having to process thoughts about my image. I felt fat and thought that I would never lose weight. Today, you can't keep my face away from the camera. Anybody who knows me knows that I have pictures of myself on my desk, in my house, everywhere.

I have been on the weight loss and gain cycle. What makes me feel good about myself is knowing that I am capable of maintaining a well-proportioned body; I just need to keep toning. I am not fat but *phat*. People shocked me when they would say that they would die for my shape. When dieting, women would say 'please, don't lose that shape.' I was complaining about something that others wanted. Now this is funny, one day my cousin's girlfriend said, "You don't know what to do with all of that; I need your body to show you what you're working with." I laughed but I was flattered.

An insecure person doesn't have to remain insecure. You can work on being secure about yourself. It really is possible to change. I am living proof. If it can happen for me, it can happen for you; I am no different from you. There is no shame in having insecurities. The shame comes when you realize that you have allowed others to make you feel insecure. When you don't fight against insecurities, you will stay stuck. You can start fighting by just praying and reading. God's word and inspirational books will empower you.

Once I realized that I had insecurities, I started to do something about it. Don't get me wrong, it was a long road to travel and heavy loads to carry, but it was worth traveling and carrying, because now I see where my confidence has gotten me today.

I pray that God, the source of hope, will fill you completely with joy and peace because you trust in him. Then you will overflow with confidence and hope. Through the power of the Holy Spirit.—Romans 15:13 (KJV)

"Your Deliverance is Coming!"

CHAPTER 4

How to Overcome Depression

*T*he hippocampus is the part of your brain that controls your emotions and your memory. Spiritual Warfare starts in the mind, and I truly believe that is where Satan goes to war against your soul.

My depression started years ago, probably in my mother's womb. You see my mother's Mom and Dad suffered with it; that is what I was told. I noticed the depression when I was ten. I didn't know what to call it, but I felt a deep sadness in my heart. I could feel the pain in my heart, and confusion in my mind. By my Mom leaving me and being raped shortly thereafter, was the main factor. Negative thoughts about my family and myself weighed heavily upon me. In this season of my life, Satan was real and active in my brain. I was battling with feelings that I couldn't talk about. As I got older, the depression worsened. I sat in the dark and cried for no reason; I also cried while listening to sad music, which put me in a deeper depressive state. No one knew of the depression because I hid it with a smile regardless of what was going on inside of me. One day, I went on a field trip with my little cousin, Marquise, as his chaperone. I was twenty-one at the time.

I sat at the table with other chaperones and watched the teacher organize everything before we left. There was a woman who sat next to me, and she began talking about God, so my ears opened up. She also stated that she was a prophet. This meant she has a gift from God and can see some future events. I didn't believe her, and I don't know why, maybe because I never met anyone who possessed the gift. Therefore, I asked her to tell me something about myself if she was really a prophet, and she did. She said, "When you are alone you cry a lot." I was in pure shock, truly. I was asking a million questions after that. She told me what spiritual gifts God had given me, and I was going to get married. I believed everything she said up until the married part. I couldn't believe that part, but it was true, and I am married today.

How do you overcome depression? You first must know that you are depressed. Some people aren't aware of it even though the signs are there. Depression can have a negative impact on your body. You may gain weight or lose weight; I have experienced both. Depression can take away your glow, that beam of light that shines so bright in you if you don't get a grip on it.

In order to overcome depression, for me, I had to become creative; I had to find something to do with my pain. I would always pray to God and cry out to Him about my troubles, and every time I cried I felt a little bit stronger. I started writing this book, and then poetry. I would go dancing a lot just to release some of the stress in my mind. I produced a documentary to help me separate from the depression that used to have me sitting in one spot for hours thinking about things I didn't have the power to change. I would read the Serenity prayer a lot, and that is why my daughter's name is Serenity. I had to accept the things that I could not change, and change the things that I could, and have the wisdom to know the difference! Those words are profound. In my life, I was trying to change things that couldn't be changed regardless of how hard I tried.

Accepting what has transpired in your life, due to bad decision making on your part or on behalf of others who mistreated you, is a necessary step in the healing process. I told my Dad I believe depression is the culprit to illness, which he suffered due to my rape and the death of his mother. His mother passed away before he had a chance to speak to her. He was told that his Mom needed to rest. She really did rest; she is resting until the trumpet sounds and resurrection takes place.

Depression can make you sick both mentally and physically. When I felt depression coming upon me, I distracted myself by engaging in different activities. I refuse to let it take over my life. As a result, my daughter would suffer because she didn't see the glow in her mommy's eyes. She needs my undivided attention in her life.

For three days, I was thinking about my mother. On Sunday, I told my Dad I should call her. The next day my mother called me. I told her that I was thinking about her. She expressed feelings of depression. My response was "God is our provider." We conversed about how depression affected our family. I used to sit in the dark and cry, so I understand the curse of depression.

I asked my Mom to move to D.C., throw away her depression medicine, and let me be her medicine. I said, "When I am feeling depressed, I do things to make me happy, *period.*" I dance, sing, write, or read. Depression is a dark place. You feel hopeless and drained. I believe that is what happened to my grandfather; depression got the best of him, and his life was cut short. I never got the opportunity to meet him, but I heard he was a very kind and humble man. My Mom was a daddy's girl just as I am with my Dad.

Depression is a form of abuse, mental agony, and aggravation. When the victim of abuse doesn't take the necessary steps to seek help or remove themselves from the situation, nothing changes. Depression kept me in this situation for years. Let me explain, I ended up in a physically abusive relationship. It began at the age of fifteen when I lost my virginity to a boy named Joseph. The main reason for giving him my virginity was due to my insecurities. I felt that if I didn't have sex with him another female would, and I wanted to keep my Boo. So for eight years, he and I were in an on and off relationship. In the last two years of the relationship, he was physically abusive. I was twenty when the abuse began and it lasted for two years. For some reason, I felt that because I was fighting him back, the situation wasn't so bad. He created a monster inside of this church girl. I was no longer afraid to fight back as I was as a kid. I would tell myself, "I am not a punk!" Being a punk didn't have anything to do with my accepting domestic violence. My self-worth diminished. Depression set in, but I kept on smiling and fighting.

One day we were both home relaxing and watching a movie on TV, I cried because the storyline hit home. The movie showed a daughter and mother reuniting. Joseph came into the room and asked why I was crying. I told him it was because I could relate to the movie. He left the room, and when he returned, he had a super-size cup full of juice in his hand and approached the bed. Out of nowhere, he threw the juice on me while I was in the bed with my PJ's on. He felt as if I was being a punk, a crybaby, and it irritated him to the point of disrespecting me. We started fighting like two strangers in the street; it was horrible. He kicked in the TV screen and snatched all of the phone cords out of the sockets. He then stole my car keys and left.

This was the worst fight ever, and the situation spilled over into another relationship that was valuable to me, but his demons were all around me. My attitude changed drastically. I changed from the sweet church girl that I use to be, to a born again fighter. The relationship added to the depression I was already battling. Nevertheless, I am a fighter. Through the years, I decided to fight for my happiness and overcome depression.

Presently, I am a domestic violence advocate. I noticed that depression plays a big role in domestic violence, and women staying with their abusers. Two main reasons are low self-esteem and fear of being alone.

Live your life, you only get one. Overcome depression today!

"Your Deliverance is Coming!"

CHAPTER 5

Relationships

*T*his chapter covers the many relationships in my life. Intimate, family, school, work, church, you name it I will discuss it. I have had so many relationships with so many people on different levels that I would have to write another book to address them all. If I had a relationship with you, God sent us on that path together— good, bad or indifferent. I truly believe that one of the purposes in my life is to build relationships with people and share wisdom. Everyone's purpose in life differs from one another. I have a purpose in life and so do you. While building relationships within my circle, I learned and taught life skills. People will come and go; those who remain were meant to stay. Some people come into my life for a season and others are there for a lifetime. I need to know the forecast more clearly, because I get confused with those who are not there for a lifetime as opposed to the ones who are. I wait upon God to show me which season I am in, and for what purpose do people serve who enter my life. In this way, I will know how to position them in my life when we first meet.

My first relationship is with God, my Creator. I was formally introduced to God when I was ten years old. I sang in the children's choir when I was five years old. It wasn't until I was baptized in water that I really began to sense His presence. It is a loving and calm feeling that I still feel today, through my mind, body, and soul. Sometimes it feels like an electric shock to my body, or a tingling sensation when I worship him. Whether I'm in the shower, car, or just about anywhere, His presence is felt. I know He is here and watching over me. My relationship with God is real, and He talks to me in the midst of my sin, or any other situations He doesn't approve of.

God knows that I know He loves me, and at the end of the day, He is all I have. This awareness affects my relationship with others in a positive way. As I put my trust and faith in Him, I feel emotionally secure and free from being ensnared in unpredictable human behavior. My relationship with God is deep, but I too must strengthen the relationships with the people I claim to love. Sometimes I feel like an abusive partner who neglects God. Like any abuser who pleads, they are sorry and never again would cause you pain, I compare this scenario to my own life, knowing full well that I hurt the heart of God when I don't forgive or when I act out in my flesh and thoughts. I hurt Him because He wants me to love people no matter what. I do practice this principle most of the time, but during others, I just don't feel like it. Relationships can have possessive qualities in terms of I belong to Him and He belongs to me, period, and nobody is going to get in the way of what we feel for one another. That is how I feel about my Creator!

When I lived alone, I would sit at my table and light dinner candles symbolic of eating dinner with God as if He was sitting right in front of me. I would talk to Him. God has always been my all. I remember being at the bottom, and I mean the very bottom in life, and He lifted me up high above everything which pertained to the situation.

Was I a perfect angel? No! Did I do everything God told me to do? No! However, my heart is pure and innocent, and God knows. My faith has increased in certain areas. God understands me. He knows there is a little girl inside of me that didn't get a chance to grow properly and understand true natural emotions. My emotions were tampered with at a very early age. Therefore, my deliverance has been and is still, coming.

There would be no me without God. This book wouldn't exist if it weren't for the Lord on my side. I may be hard-headed about certain things, but I have felt my spankings, and my blessings come straight from Heaven. My relationship with my earthly Dad is similar but different. We always spend quality time together, and I feel safe with him even in his illness.

My Daughter

My relationship with my daughter is special. When Serenity was born in 2007, I knew she would be unique. After delivery, she was cleansed by the doctor and laid across my chest with her back on my stomach, Serenity didn't cry but looked at me as if to say, "Mommy, I am here, are you ready?" From day one, I always spoke to her as if she could understand me. I would have conversations with her before she could eat solid food. Serenity became very expressive, smart, and witty, to the point of standing firm on technical issues and challenging issues she feels is unjust. She is a young advocate. I foresee it already.

Shortly before I was married, when Serenity was five years old, my husband, Serenity, and I were in my room. I sat on the floor organizing DVD's with David, my husband, prior to our marriage. It may have been six months before the wedding. Anyway, David was sitting in a chair while Serenity was sitting on the bed. Serenity looked at me and said, "Mommy, do you want to marry David?" I said, "Yes!" She looked at David and said, "Do you want to marry my mom," and he said, "Yes!" She summoned us to her side, "Come here," and she opened her arms. David was under her left arm and me under her right arm; she hugged us around our neck. David started laughing and said, "Serenity, you are choking me." Without a smile on her face and portraying a serious demeanor, she looked at him, then looked up to the ceiling and said, "Yes, yes, yes, yes." Then she said, "Y'all can go now." My husband and I looked at each other and said, "Did she just marry us?"

We still believe Serenity married us before we took our vows in the church. This was an example of her uniqueness. However, there are moments when I am caught off guard with some of her expressive comments.

On another occasion, I felt stunned by the words that came out of her mouth so I kept quiet. Out of the clear blue sky, she said, "I am going to miss you when you die, Mommy." She said the same thing about her stepfather then she said, "I am going to miss myself when I die, too. I know we all have to go up in the sky with God one day."

On another note, Serenity likes the type of music that airs on an old school music station. Her rhythm to the music is like someone who used to dance back in the day. Our relationship is defined by love and we love each other very much. Sometimes, she will hug and kiss me so much that I run from her. She is over the top; she will pin me down and not let go and I just laugh. We laugh often. It's good for the soul.

I taught Serenity about God, who He is, and why we pray to Him. Being in tune with her spiritual side, she anointed my head with olive oil and prayed for me. She battles the evil spirits that come around. She said, "Mommy, I hate the devil because he put bad things in my head; I want him to die." I told her that when he puts bad thoughts in her head she just needs to say, "Leave me alone in Jesus' name," and to scream those words if she has to, but just don't give in. I have always been real with my daughter. I told her Mommy is not here to stay, but while I am on this earth I need her to remember what I taught her, e.g., trust in the Lord and know that He will always be there for you.

I am raising a soul sister. I taught her about our African American culture. She has gone on trips to see black history exhibits and we watched numerous slavery documentaries. Also, we visited the library to research books about Civil Rights. My baby is equipped with knowledge and thoroughly educated when it comes to understanding her culture. I believe God gave Serenity to me to help me mature and understand the virtue of patience. She is also very helpful and creative. A documentary was birthed in me two months after I gave birth to Serenity. Years passed while working on the documentary. One day I put the documentary aside to attend other obligations. Serenity came to the rescue. My baby went into the studio and was my motivation while working on the documentary. She became my support system. I noticed two months after she was born my creativity increased and I was more innovative. In 2012, Serenity, my husband, and I went to a prayer night service at church. The pastor and his wife walked around the entire church praying for everyone. When my pastor reached Serenity, he touched her and removed his hand quickly, as if he was electrocuted. He said, "This is a special one right here. She is a special one who has a special gift and she will have a lot of haters because of it. Keep her grounded in the Word and she will be just fine." I started crying and Serenity did too. On the day I gave birth to Serenity I knew she was unique, but I had no idea that God had given her extra special gifts. Jesus loves you Serenity and so do I!

My Husband

I met my husband at Ally's wedding, one of the sisters I adopted as my own. I was one of the bridesmaids, and he was a groomsman for his cousin. I didn't notice him until the reception, but he said that he noticed me when I stepped out of the bridesmaid's line and read a scripture. He was curious on how much knowledge I had about the spiritual realm. While on the dance floor at the reception, he danced near me. I acknowledged him by saying, "I see you." Then I smiled, and he came closer because he felt welcomed into my space. He pulled me closer, but I backed away. He said he didn't mean any harm, I believed him, and we kept dancing. When the song was over I walked away, but he followed me. He asked, "Are you coming back?" I smiled and expressed 'maybe' with my facial expression. I really wasn't coming back and I didn't want to agree verbally. So, if I didn't return, I never gave my word and therefore, I wasn't accountable for the disappearing act.

I was so happy that my friend was married. I was not thinking about meeting my future husband at her wedding. I was at a place in my life where I was content with just being one with myself. I slipped away to go to the bridal room in the Newton Mansion with one of my friends and the godmother of the bride. As we sat chatting, we heard a knock on the door, and it was my husband. He said, "Hey, my name is David, and I am just getting home from the Army. I would like to give you my number so I can get to know you a little better." I looked at him and smiled because he was so meek, like a dove. He further stated that he is a military man who just completed eight years in the Army and had been to Iraq twice. My curiosity escalated because I always had boyfriends, guys that had an edge with them, who were never meek. However, this man was truly the opposite, in my opinion. If he survived the Iraq war, then surely this was enough edge for me.

Many women want a man who can stand up and protect them. I accepted his number and gave him mine. I found out that he was an Aquarius just like me; this was so interesting to me, another water child. I told him very personal things about myself on our first date because I didn't want to waste his time. I wanted him to know who I was and what I was about early so he could decide if he really wanted to stick around. He also did the same, which shocked me, because men like to keep secrets. I believe we were both tired of being a sheep amongst wolves. We wanted to expose ourselves early, so later on down the road we wouldn't feel surprised at what we may see in each other.

He called me the next day, and I asked him one hundred questions. He answered some questions, but not all. I understood because I was digging for gold; I wanted to know all about Iraq. My perception of men in the military was different from his character. We dated for months before I introduced him to Serenity; they met at my cousin's church. Serenity was three years old. My husband said he remembered the look in her eyes when she met him. It was a look that signified, you and my Mom are going to be more than friends. As time passed, I slowly allowed him to interact with my family because I was unsure of where the relationship was going. I sensed he was a genuinely nice person that I would always be friends with regardless of the outcome. He recognized my loyalty. I never discussed topics to anyone that were shared between us and I never will. Loyalty means a lot to me. It is worth more than money to me. I have street smarts, understand the seriousness of words, and I know how they travel to strange places. David trusted me as a friend and now he was ready for love, but I wasn't ready.

Why? It took me longer to prepare for marriage because my pain was deep, so deep that love didn't live here anymore. In my eyes, love had failed me, and God was all I needed in that season of my life. Nothing was able to penetrate my heart; not gifts, money, intimacy, or the selfless service that he always provided. Because of my many life experiences, I didn't want love to mess it up as I felt it had based on the past. One day my husband said, "Do you think God would bring me into your life to hurt you or Serenity?" He answered the question for me, "No!"

On September 11, 2012, after dating for two-and-a-half years. I finally let my guard down and let him in my heart. David, Serenity, and I were sitting at the dinner table and we prayed as we always do before eating. Suddenly, David excused himself from the table and returned with a small box. He got on one knee and asked me if he could have the honor of being my husband. I said, "Yes." On May 25, 2013, we were married. The prophecy that was given to me concerning marriage over ten years ago finally came to pass. I have a husband. My family loves him; my friends do too. Serenity calls him daddy and tells him that she loves him, and I think that's special. God spoke to me in so many ways and through people. I began to feel safe. That hurt little undone person in me, was free to love again, but this time it was not counterfeit. I love you King David!

My Biological Sister and Brother

I wasn't raised with my biological sister and brother; therefore, we really didn't get the opportunity to bond. Nevertheless, I love them because they are my siblings. I reach out to them by phone as much as possible. My brother didn't find out about me until he was fifteen years old; my sister knew about me, and saw me for the first time when she was fourteen years old. WOW! What a coincidence, right? My brother lives in Richmond; my sister lives in New York, and I live in D.C. What we share together is being birthed from our Mother's womb, we are connected for life. I wish that we all grew up together but we didn't. I pray and hope that we have a closer relationship and are able to spend quality time with one another. We all have children that haven't met and God knows it is time. My sister and I have spent more time together compared to my brother. I visited her in New York on a few occasions, and she has traveled to D.C to visit me. My brother came to my daughter's birthday party when she turned two years old. I haven't seen him in a while, but we do communicate by phone. He is so wise; I feel like the little sister and he is the big brother. He truly amazes me with the profound sayings that proceed from his mouth. I know that God answers prayers and we will all come together soon.

School days at Shaw Junior High and Cardozo Senior High

I have friends from junior high and senior high school whom I continue to interact with. When I attended Shaw Junior High, I loved my school; what I didn't like was one rule, which prevented us from bringing candy to school. I loved eating candy; I would buy them by the pack. I had a good relationship with a young lady named Yvette. She was a ray of sunshine to me. She always had my back, even though we didn't spend a lot of quality time together after school. She lived in Clifton, a neighborhood near Cardozo. I sent her a picture from our yearbook recently to remind her of our years at Cardozo. I also had a friend named

Sabrina. She was there for me at a very critical time in my life. I was there for her too. However, when she became friends with Yvette our friendship dwindled. I was cool with that because sometimes that happens and I have learned to accept it. I still love her! When I reminisce about my high school years, I really enjoyed it and the people I met. Like my high school friend Shaun and I, we hung in a group; it was seven of us. We called ourselves the "To Fly Homies." It sounded cute to us, but it really meant that we all were fly by working and accomplishing things in life. I was the person that everyone liked. There were female groups who opposed each other. However, I remained in a neutral position. So, do you know what I learned? I learned to say "No" to transfer information. I knew specific details about both groups but refused to gossip. No one could say, "Kisha said this or that" because I learned in high school that gossip travels fast. I dropped the ball once, and it wasn't good, so I made a vow never to fall victim to gossiping again!

My Work

I started working at a government office in 1996. I was in the eleventh grade, and I was offered a summer job through Cardozo Trans-Tech program. The program helped students learn administrative skills in preparation for the workforce. On our first day of work, I and other students were escorted to the auditorium. My assignment was to work in human resources, but this woman stood up and said, "We need somebody in our office." I call her Ms. Wonderful. She asked to have me, little old me, as her summer aide. I believe in the phrase "a ram in the bush." I also believe that God has people in place to get you to the next level. I worked throughout the summer. In my senior year of high school, I was rehired. I worked and went to school part-time.

Ms. Wonderful eventually created a permanent position in her office for me. One week after graduating from school, I went to work full-time. Not only was I blessed with a job, I was given the opportunity to work in the administrator's support office. This enabled me to see how the agency operated from the top to bottom. I was responsible for logging in all of the memos, and opening and acquiring signatures on documents for the administrator. I also researched Freedom of Information Act requests and was assigned other duties.

Ms. Wonderful mentored me. She taught me how to dress professionally, and how to display my temperament in a work environment. Ms. Wonderful possessed strong and focused character traits; she wasn't involved in cliques as most folks in the building were. She did her work and mentored me. Because of her grooming, I wear makeup and perfume. Remember, my Dad raised me, so I had to learn other dimensions of being a young woman. Therefore, God used her to lead the way. As time passed, other women helped me too. I have met many people on the job, different personalities, from different backgrounds.

At my work, angels and demons really do look alike. There are people who have rubbed me the right way; they really are angels, and others who have rubbed me the wrong way, by revealing my secrets and trying to make a mockery out of me. Appearing as an angel of light, my free-spirited soul was lead into a web of deception.

On a better note, I started working in another office with Inez and Israel. They pushed me to the next level in my career. I was given a travel credit card so I could travel with them to attend conferences. We have traveled to Texas, Los Angeles, and New Jersey. They were instrumental in helping me evolve by instructing me to enroll in training courses. I took a few courses at a community college.

God blessed me because I did what He asked me to do. I don't always obey; that is just my human nature, but I am so glad that I listened to my Heavenly Father. Working in a new office has helped me to mature in many areas. Inez, my director at the time, was such a wonderful person to work for; she didn't play games. Inez was a queen and a great leader; she invested in my growth and had my best interest at heart. Israel, my manager, exuded a calm disposition and was very precise. I like how he carries himself. I respected them both. In my opinion, our relationship was wonderful. However, Inez retired, and I cried just as I did when Ms. Wonderful retired. These were two strong black women whom I admired for all of their hard work and dedication to helping another young woman strive for excellence. I am grateful for all my work experiences, because it has made me smarter and wiser. I have learned to cut the grass low so that I can see the snakes. I never let the snakes know that I cut the grass, they find out when they get into the garden.

I have learned many lessons pertaining to the working environment. I never tried to fit in with anyone, I was always me, regardless of whether I was accepted or not. Oftentimes, I tried to figure out why people have so much hate and envy inside. It is due to low-esteem or lack of personal development, which prevents a person from being happy.

I have built beautiful relationships with people. Some began well, and ended differently, like a beautiful rose that has sat on someone's desk for a week with no water. Still, I continue to love people and let them fit in where they belong in my life.

The relationship I have with my mentor Asia is vital. She was placed in my life to show me how to be a professional. I like how she carries herself, and how dedicated she is. She works hard at any given task. She gives me instructions to help me in my endeavors. In this appointed season in my life, I realize it is up to me to follow the instructions that are given, whether it's advice for home or work. I had many mentors in different seasons of my life, and I apply their wisdom when I deem it necessary.

Asia is a wise and strong woman. I asked God to bring strong women and the brave at heart into my circle, and He has. Every woman who walks closely with me is a soldier. I am not saying that they don't hurt or go through tough times, or need a shoulder to cry on; they just know how to bounce back from the burdens women have to deal with in life.

God had blessed her with many gifts, yet, He has only revealed two of them to me. I see one that is used for me on a regular basis. Thank you Lord. Asia is the type of woman that some women have a problem with or keep a distance. Because she keeps a low profile, some women can't figure her out. She is pretty, smart, humble, and possess a professional demeanor. One day Asia and I were talking, and she told me that her niece, Cupcake, had lied to her about something and continued to lie after Asia knew she wasn't telling the truth. By the look on her face, Asia was upset. She told me never to lie to her. I was smiling because I told her straight up she doesn't have to worry about that with me. When I start relationships with people I tell them upfront about me, and how I am. I will tell you nothing before I would lie. I pray that everybody takes heed to my words. I don't expect to be lied to either; my Dad made it very clear about the dangers of lying. I felt that this conversation took place because she was very disappointed and upset with someone that she loves, therefore, she didn't ever want to feel that from me.

I am glad my mentor is giving me the opportunity to show her that I am a trustworthy person. I have realized in my relationships with people, that sometimes people have had bad experiences with people, this can make things hard for the new kid on the block. Willie Lynch said, "Distrust is greater than trust." As African Americans, we sometimes don't trust one another or give a person a chance, before we start labeling them, based on behaviors of people that have betrayed our trust in the past; everybody is different. I have more people who trust me than those who distrust me. Those who know me see the truth in me. You can't have a healthy relationship with anyone if you don't trust him or her. I don't have relationships with people I don't trust anymore; I use to, but my life is less stressful and I can still love with AGAPE love from a distance; it is a waste of my energy trying to distinguish what is the truth or a lie; God reveals to me whom I can trust and can't with certain things. I never thought to ask Him in the past about who is trustworthy; I thought I knew but I didn't.

Where I work presently, enables me to help people by providing information that promotes business growth. I have a passion for helping people in any way that I can, which is a part of my personality.

Sometimes I think that hate has been the force that caused my guiding light to shine and maintain a positive outlook within. I am a liberal free-spirited young woman with a radiant personality. To my surprise, this doesn't go over so well with others. I would think others would join the bandwagon if they feel otherwise.

I get that shine even when I am down or discouraged. The Holy Spirit rises up in me and gives me hope. It surprises me that I still have love and forgiveness in my heart for those who have wronged me. I have come to the conclusion in life, "It's okay to be me." God is truly worth keeping. He hasn't failed me yet.

My Path with Females

I tend to run into women who struggle just like me, abused women, women who have been hurt by men, or in other ways. I am a direct person, for many reasons, yet, gentle and meek as an infant." It frustrates me sometimes when I have to explain my behavior to my foes. Sometimes I don't care if they think certain things about me and sometimes I do. I guess that is a part of maturity. I often wonder if I am patient enough with people. I have come a long way. Shaun and I have been best friends since we were both five, and she was the only friend that I truly loved. Now, I have a whole slew of friends and extended family that I love equally. Each of my relationships is different, but my love is the same, it is called acceptance. There are those in my life that I chose to deal with, based on who they are and what they brought to the table, as they walked with me. I don't have to accept everybody's past and what it created in them, but I do.

I am the chosen one in my circle of friends to help women rebuild their trust with other women. That is what I tell everybody. I am the only one who can carry this torch, nobody else but me during this season of my life. Nobody would have the patience to care about another woman's feelings or to be the glue that keeps the relationship consistent. I don't know one person in my circle that would put up with all of the different emotions that I have had to put up with. How do I do it? The love of God keeps me loving them, even when my flesh doesn't want to be bothered. Sometimes I feel like disappearing for a while, staying to myself and focusing on me, but I don't. I can't because my heart will not let me. I was called to be a leader and not a follower. Now don't get me wrong, in order to be a successful leader you have to be able to follow and humble yourself enough to take instructions from others in an authority position. Have I ever buckled authority? Yes. I also realized that in the end I still didn't win whatever situation I was fighting, unless I was fighting to save my sanity. I have walked in the footsteps of Moses, not exactly, but in terms of leading others who felt hopeless, without strength or oppressed. As the old saying goes, 'if the shoe fits, wear it.' I am putting my soul on these pages, so let's be real right now with ourselves. There have been times that we thought we could fight this fight called "life no good." However, at the end of the day, Jesus is a healer, and he will heal the brokenhearted if you ask Him to and you believe that He will answer your prayer. I have seen the brokenness and the success of women. In both situations, we need one another.

My First Boyfriend

I previously wrote about my relationship with Joseph. Now, I will tell you how the story ends. Remember, I grew up as a church girl, and he grew up in the rough part of Southeast in D.C., and he didn't attend church.

I was twenty-three when he exited my life. I suffered domestic violence in the relationship, and it became obvious to my friends, family, and coworkers.

An incident occurred when I threatened to leave him after a night of arguing. He called me at work the next day and said, "Come downstairs

Kisha; I want to talk to you." He was calm. I told Ms. Wonderful that I was running out front for a moment and I would be right back. He was waiting for me out front in my car. When I got into the car, he pulled off; I was hysterical to say the least. "Where are you taking me, I have to go back to work?"

He said, "You are not leaving me; I am taking you home." Oh my goodness, I couldn't believe this foolishness. I went into panic mode and while the car was in motion, I grabbed the gear and put the car in park mode. I convinced him to take me back to work. He was so scared to lose me, but he didn't know how to love me properly. Love is not possessive. He then reached over and bit me so hard on my face that his teeth marks left a print. I had to move my hair to the other side of my face to cover up the teeth marks. My coworkers thought something was bizarre; I rearranged my hair in the middle of the day.

He kidnapped me, and I did what I had to do to keep from being fired and get back to my job. I told him that I wouldn't leave him and that we could stay together. I said this just so he would free me so I could go back to work. At 4:30 p.m., Joseph was waiting for me outside. I played it off as if nothing ever happened because I knew he was emotional.

I started planning my escape. In my mind, I had already left him, but I had to leave physically. We fought every other day and the fights were brutal. I would fight him back, but I was getting tired.

We stayed together and the fighting continued. One night I was in the bed asleep and all of a sudden, I felt somebody jump on me. I woke up to find nobody there, but I was being held down by something that I couldn't see, I was in shock for a second. I could only move my head; I looked at Joseph sleeping and tried to call out to him, but I couldn't talk either. I knew what to do next, so I did it; I called on Jesus! I started saying Jesus under my breath. I began to say his name aloud again and again, Jesus, Jesus, Jesus, Jesus, Jesus, until that evil spirit released me. I read about demons in the Bible but on that night, I was faced with one.

Once it let me go, I ran into the bathroom and sat on the floor in disbelief. I had never experienced anything like that before in my life. It confirmed the demons I felt around me. I was living in sin, too, so they were really taking advantage of the situation.

One day I stayed home from work; my body and soul was weary. I was ill. Joseph had a temporary job at the time, so he wasn't home. I lay on my bed, looked up to the ceiling, and asked God please help me get out of this crazy unhealthy relationship. I told God that I knew I put myself in this situation and I was sorry. About five months later, God answered my prayers. You never know how God will deliver you out of the situation. It was a Saturday morning in the winter, and Tonya who has always prayed for me, gave me a pair of PJ's that I wore that day; it looked like a baby sleeper. The only parts you could see were my head and my hands. Joseph was so irritated at the sight of it. He wanted me to take it off, so he said, "Boo, come on, let's have sex." I said, "No, I am not having sex with you anymore, I am not married. I can't do this anymore." He said, "What, you're not doing this anymore?" He stated that since I started going to a new church, I began changing. I adapted to new ways of living that began to transform my life for the better. Backsliders, like I was, go in and out of this stage. We wake up and come back like the prodigal son. He had the nerve to put my Bible in the oven and turn it on. I was in pure shock, and I said, "You are in trouble now."

He totally flipped the script. (A saying my Dad uses). I was sitting on the couch and he started breaking every mirror in the apartment. His face changed like a monster. Then he picked up my glass centerpiece from the table and proceeded to bust me over the head with it. I crossed my legs and looked at him with so much peace in my heart, and told him to go ahead and do what he had to do because I would be free from him. My attitude was, 'Give me freedom or give me death' because I am out of here today. He really tried to crack me in the head with the glass, but it was as if a force was preventing him from doing it. He started crying and then turned around and tackled me to the ground, ripped my pajamas off, and raped me. I was disgusted, frustrated, and hurt. I was feeling every emotion imaginable.

My soul was empty. I started to feel numb all over, no emotions anymore, no thoughts, just a blank screen. He said, "Boo, I am sorry. It was like he snapped back from another person. I am going to church with you tomorrow." I just grabbed the broom and started cleaning up the glass as if I was the only person in the apartment. He said he was going over my aunt's house and he would see me later. He also told me that he loved me. As soon as he left, I called Tonya who had given me the PJ's and told her that I needed somewhere to stay because I couldn't do this anymore. She welcomed me, and I packed all of my clothes and personal stuff and left. When Joseph got home and saw that my clothes and shoes were gone, he lost his mind, I am sure of it. He kept calling my cell phone but I wouldn't answer. Monday was a holiday, so he had to wait until Tuesday to get in touch with me at work.

Tuesday morning at eight, my phone rang from a number that I didn't recognize. It was him on the other end. "Where have you been?" he asked. I told him not to worry about it because we were done for good, I was not coming back. I faxed over a thirty-day notice to the rental office, so I could properly vacate the apartment. I was done! He said, "Bring my social security card and my birth certificate downstairs or I am coming up to your office to get it." I believed him because he had managed to use the pay phone in the lobby; he had gotten past the guards. I called my coworker, Tyson, he was like a brother to me, who knew about my situation, so he accompanied me downstairs. He was older than I was and married. He tried to mentor Joseph at one time, but that didn't work out very well. We went outside and saw Joseph sitting by the metro elevator across the street.

I handed him his belongings, and he said, "Why did you bring your play brother out here?" Then he grabbed me by my shirt and ripped every button on it. Tyson grabbed him and slammed him to the ground. Tyson told me afterward that he saw something evil in his face as he popped up off the ground. As I was walking, I said, "I hate you." I started walking toward the building, holding my shirt together, and out of nowhere I heard two of my friends from the building say, "Run, Kisha, run, he is coming!" I started running because the way they called out to me was as if my life was in danger, so I assumed he had a weapon in his hand. I didn't look back; I just ran. Not long after, something in me told me to stop running and I did. I stopped, turned around, and said, "Satan, what do you want from me?" He replied, "I don't know." Then he turned around and ran away. The security guard came outside and the federal police were called. I remember someone at work gave me a sweater to put on, and I went to the D.C. Court building and filed a restraining order against him.

I went to work the next day with my head held high because I was free from him, and people didn't know my story so they just gossiped and I let them. I was alive; I was free from him, and that was all I cared about. I felt like a slave on that remarkable day in 1865 when my ancestors were freed. I also needed to understand that my bondage was over. About an hour after I got to work, the phone rang, and I asked my team leader to answer it and if it was Joseph, to tell him that I wasn't in. Lo and behold, it was him. She answered and did what I asked of her, and he told her that she was a liar. He then called again and my co-worker answered. Before she could say that I wasn't in, he told her that he had broken into my apartment and that he was going to kill himself in there. The look on her face was that of pure fear and her hands were shaking as she hung up the phone. She told me and Ms. Wonderful what he said and Ms. Wonderful told me to call the Prince George County Suicide squad. I said, "Why? Let him do it, if he is that miserable, please let him go ahead, because I am tired." When a woman is fed up it is a wrap, *period*, it is done with no emotions behind it. This is when you know it is done and over with because there are no more emotions involved. Ms. Wonderful wanted me to think logically and be mature about this situation. She told me that was the wrong answer, and I didn't want that to happen in my apartment. I called PG and they told me that I would have to meet them at the apartment to let them in.

I caught a taxi home. I was pissed. When I arrived, the police were there surrounding the apartment building. Joseph had the couch barricaded to the door. The police forced their way into the apartment as I watched from outside.

After speaking with Joseph, an officer returned to say that he was very disturbed about our breakup and that they had to handcuff him to a chair. I really didn't care at this point. Because we both were young, the officer didn't take the nature of this incident seriously. He advised us to talk out our differences. Talk about what? I told them that I was on my way back to work. The police uncuffed Joseph and left.

As I proceeded to the bus stop, I looked back. Joseph was standing in front of the window, drawing a heart with his hands signifying he loved me. I kept on going.

Free at last! I was free and God answered my prayers.

> *"And here's what I'm saying:*
> *Ask and you'll get;*
> *Seek and you'll find;*
> *Knock and the door will open."*—Luke 11:9

I truly believe God answered my prayer. Joseph and I had to end it. Knowing me, I would have gone back to him eventually, if he didn't cause a scene at my job. Thank you, Lord. I was brainwashed into thinking about the love that I thought we shared. Every moment I think about the hell I went through with Joseph, I thank God that I survived. Now, I am a domestic violence advocate for the Lakeisha Brown Foundation. Because of my experience with domestic violence, it is real and people need to understand how serious it is. I truly thank Mignon Anderson for her dedication to the cause by starting this foundation in her daughter's name. She lost her teenage daughter due to domestic violence.

Two years after this foolishness took place Joseph called me at work. "Hey Kisha, I was working in the area and wanted to see you. I am outside." It was ten minutes prior to quitting time. I prayed before going outside; he had a big smile on his face. I didn't feel as if I were in danger. I asked him how was he doing and he said well. I asked him to walk with me to the reflection pool by the Capital and he did. We sat by the water and I asked him if he wanted to be saved and I explained to him what being saved meant. He said yes. I asked him to repeat after me, *"Lord, forgive me of my sins, and I welcome you in my life as my savior from this day forth!"* I said, "you are saved now, no matter what goes on in your life now the Lord will be with you." He then started to tell me how the demons took a hold of him and why he abused women. All I can say is that he blamed his mother for some horrific things that had happened to him and, after all of these years, he finally revealed it to me.

My Sisters

I adopted nine sisters who range from ages thirty to fifty-five. We endured life's challenges and stuck by each other's side. When you feel genuine love, you know it is real. I am blessed with a great support system, which brings tears to my eyes. We genuinely love each other. There is no judgment, hostility, or dysfunction in our relationships. Being transparent is one of the benefits I get to enjoy with them; I can be Lakisha, Kisha, and Smiley (which is my ID, my ego, and super ego). Outside of them, I treat every relationship accordingly because I know people from all walks of life; from the minister to the business owner, the police, physiologist, and the stripper; the list goes on. I have learned in life that not everything is for everybody, so I try not to mix my relationships with one another. Shaun is in a league of her own because I have known her since I was five; she was the only one there when my life was nothing but crazy and painful. Shaun was around before I became the person I am today; she suffered with me. Even though I hesitated to use the words, "I love you," I felt it in my heart. Now, I say it all the time to Shaun and all those whom I love. Shaun and I were a pair; you would always see us together. Now we have children and jobs to go to, but our friendship is solid, this sistership is forever. All of my sisters bring something unique and special to my life; I believe God handpicked them for such a time as this. They are smart go-getters and they love the Lord. They do not qualify as punks; if you start anything with them, they will finish it. However, they are driven for success, and they want to live and not just exist.

I want to make sure that I address the systemic issue that I have noticed in relationships. Running. Never run during a serious non-violent issue, just walk away if you can't handle it. Never run because it is cowardly. What I mean by run is leave a situation without bringing closure to it; just packing up and running. Sometimes people run because they want to prove a point, it serves no purpose. Leave, return and deal with the issue and move on. Men have run in my life, and I was overwhelmed, but I dealt with it. Learning to communicate effectively as opposed to running away from the situation, can build healthier relationships.

I am passing on some sweet wisdom and I hope it tastes good to you. Wisdom comes from God, and He gets all the credit for the wisdom that He has given me.

Foes

In the African American community, I truly believe that some black men and women were never properly taught how to handle conflict. When I envision slavery—the beating, belittling, and foul language, it is a behavior that has passed generationally; if no one breaks it the behavior continues. This type of behavior is also seen in domestic violence situations. People will argue that all races deal with this, for now I am not focused on all races. I am focused on the Black Culture struggle. If parents have limited knowledge, it may affect their kids. Parents have to learn how to do better. Knowledge is power, and the information that you will gain from reading this book is powerful too.

The day that I close my eyes for good, this world will have known that there was an angel present. My flesh is another story and of another color, but my heart is so big that I trust people that shouldn't be trusted, my sisters know this about me. I have shared my life and my struggle with those who secretly mock me and make fun of me. Yet, I continue to smile and show no real signs of the pain they caused me. They don't even know that I am aware of it.

Just like a minister once said, "If I really saw all the snares and traps that are designed to hurt me or destroy me, I would indeed be crazy." God protects me from certain battles, and He fights them alone. The other battles He wants me involved in so that it will build character and humbleness within me.

God is not a man who would lie. I know that God loves me and that is not a lie. Some who say they love God and follow His word have deliberately hurt and mocked me too. God is not to blame. Some people are mocking Him by playing with His scripture.

I asked myself, "why am I here on this Earth and why did God want me to write this book?" It is transforming. When I look back over my life, I know there is a God in my life. He has protected me from seen and unseen things that no human being could ever have, and kept me in the palm of His hand. He uses people to help us because He is bodiless; He is a Spirit being, and He is all-powerful!

"Your Deliverance Is Coming!"

CHAPTER 6

Bondage

Enslavement, bound, captured.

$\mathcal{M}$y African American heritage is important to me. I decided to research my history and culture. This is what I have discovered. I stepped on the scene in January 1979; my understanding of what my people went through was revealed to me ten years later while visiting the Walter T. Daniel Library in Washington, D.C. This is where my journey began. I went to the second floor, grabbed a book and read about our great historical leaders, as I sat in the huge whale's mouth, which was carpeted. It was a reading area and I loved going there. I was more interested in learning about the person I would eventually see and heard about. I heard a little about our great leaders in school. In our living room, we had a picture of them. I also got the opportunity to visit the grave sight of some of the most prominent leaders in our history.

With African American leaders as pioneers, they held prestigious positions which allowed them to make a difference by spreading powerful messages to people who had the power to make change happen. So here I am a person driven by my love for my people. I would love to speak to the president. I would tell him that I am a former slave of mental slavery. I ran toward freedom from the trap that was set up for me in the streets of Washington, D.C. I decided, and believed that I must be free. Like some of my ancestors felt, *"Give me liberty or give me death"* I feel the same way which prompted this comment. (Wirt, William. Sketches of the Life and Character of Patrick David. (Philadelphia) 1836, as reproduced in The World's Great Speeches, Lewis Copeland and Lawrence W. Lamm, eds., (New York) 1973.) There are slaves waiting to be emancipated in their minds. Their minds are trapped in injustice to themselves. We have to reach out to the lost and hurting. Do you know people can be in bondage to pain and mental agony?

The pain of slavery and segregation could have allowed my brothers to give up on hope. However, Martin Luther King, Jr. and Frederick Douglas started out as regular people who had faith and courage. They had to build themselves up so they could be heard and start a movement. This is amazing and it inspires me. I am a regular person who has built myself up to create change by first releasing this book. The reason that I am so expressive about this area of bondage is because it is a pain in my side. All of the things that I have seen around me and wanted to understand are now coming to the surface. For instance, domestic violence, rape, betrayal, and all sorts of evil and more serious things began to happen.

Hurting people started hurting themselves; this is just my observation and personal research. Over the years, I am sure some of you have experienced family members who have displayed certain types of behaviors that are dysfunctional. From generation to generation, people have suffered from the residue of slavery and the cruel behavior that resulted from it. I am not saying all black families are suffering from this residue but some are. My people have been abused mentally, physically, and emotionally. Children are growing up having to search for their identity because their parents and grandparents didn't know who they really were.

"Throw Away People" was a documentary produced by Washington Media that my Dad and I were a part of in 1989. What does 'throw away'

people mean? I asked my Dad the same question in 2014, and his response was, "we African American's have been neglected and denied our full privileges and rights after building this nation with our blood, sweat, and tears. We were given slave wages after slavery ended." He felt we were just thrown away to fend for ourselves. Wow! My Dad was telling the truth, and it sounded so profound coming from him.

Our involvement with the documentary was due to the tragic death of a young man who was murdered in our neighborhood, in broad daylight while kids, including me, were outside playing. In my opinion, this act of violence was once acceptable in society toward African Americans. Nowadays, in some parts of the African American community, we are destroying each other as we were destroyed during slavery. We held a vigil for the young man on the street. I attended the gathering and volunteered to sing a song in his honor. A reporter from Washington Media was there and was astounded, by the way I sang, and because I was a young girl. She asked my Dad if I could be interviewed, and that's how we became a part of the documentary. The crime in our streets is horrific. Historically, hate groups would freely kill black people and not be convicted of a crime. Now, you have black people going around killing each other, thinking they won't get caught, but they do. Do you see the bondage?

Bondage to anything is unhealthy; it insinuates you are bound to something unwillingly, out of fear or due to a lack of knowledge. Bondage begins in the mind, it's similar to your hands, and feet being chained, rendering you void of movement. From a spiritual perspective, the scenario is the same. Over the years, I realized I was in bondage to mindsets and belief systems which hindered my personal development. The bondage represented personal experiences and exposure to environments that were established to keep a person in bondage.

Once I recognize the signs that a bound person portrays, I sit back and observe them carefully. Then, I pray and ask God to show me how to deal with the person. I have learned where to place people in my life.

I was designed to be the way I am. I often say that I was born in the wrong generation. The generation that fought for civil rights, freedom, and equality is where I belong. Although, I was born for such a time as this; I desire to see people free from pain and mental slavery. Based on my humanitarian nature, making peace with people is what I love to do, and making friends is equally important.

Mental bondage is formed when you first believe a lie. You get stuck in the mindset that is detrimental to your health, and those around you! For example, believing you can't trust anybody is paranoia. Yes, there are some people you can't trust, nor should you. That is the reality. Nevertheless, there are those you can if you put forth the effort to let them in. Distrusting the entire human race is residue from slavery or should I say the Willie Lynch letter, he stated, "Distrust is GREATER than trust so instill this into your slave, and they will always be your slave even when they are freed!" He also said "Separate the light skin slave from the dark skin slave!" Tell me why reader? He wanted to cause strife and division amongst us, thinking that one is better than the other. This deception has resonated through the African American community!

During slavery, the slave master would separate the lighter complexioned slaves from the darker complexioned slaves. This caused divisions within our own race. You had the house Negro and the field Negro.

The Willie Lynch letter startled me; I thought about everything written in that letter and the things that I see in my lifetime today. Slaves were free to go in 1865, but the stench of slavery hovered over entire generations. There are people who wouldn't welcome a dark skin baby if they had one. I heard a woman cry because she was light skin, and her husband was brown skin. She didn't want the baby to be brown/dark skin. I was shocked to witness such ignorance and thought, "What do you think of me?"

I held a color complexion event at the Thurgood Marshall Center in Washington, D.C, and the panel consisted of a dark skin panel and light skin panel with an age requirement of seventeen years-sixty-five years old. I conducted interviews prior to the event to choose my panel. They shared their experiences with me, so I concluded they were either stereotyped or mistreated because of their skin color. I posted flyers up around the facility portraying stereotypes that people sent to me when I conducted a census on Facebook. I wanted to get feedback on the issue.

My best friend, Shaun, is light skinned, and I am dark skinned, and we both have experienced discrimination within our own race; the way we are perceived is residue from the mindset of slavery, although, it didn't affect our sistership! I really want my people to be free from the bondage in their mind so that they can be free to trust and love one another without judging. At the end of the day, the God of Peace wants us to live in peace. Here are a few comments from my census:

• Dark skin people are better lovers! (Some of the slave master's that participated in raping the slave women felt the same way)

• Light skin people think that they are better! (Willie Lynch, right?)

• I only date light skin females because you can see their features better! (Insults were used a lot during slavery)

Some people fight to get free by any means necessary and some people stay bound! I rebelled against that old slave mentality by refusing to be a part of it.

One day at work, I was searching for someone to deliver a memo to. I didn't know where the offices were, so I asked for assistance to locate them. The assistant was touched by my smile and my domineering attitude. From her own lips, she uttered that I was very nice to be a dark-skinned woman. She also said that dark skin women treat her very mean and are abrupt with her when asking a question. I was filled with compassion and wanted to give her a hug, but we were strangers, we just met. We kept in touch.

Some people deceive themselves into believing they are not in bondage. I was called black, and all kind of names because of the color of my skin, even names of candy bars. Nevertheless, I didn't allow myself to be deceived nor turn on my own because of the mindsets of others.

Lastly, bondage can make you feel uncomfortable. The first step to freedom is acknowledging that you are in bondage, not necessarily due to slavery, but anything in your life that you think is holding you hostage. You could be in bondage because of unforgiveness. I understand the struggle, to get free is the hardest part but it is worth the fight! The struggle of our ancestors should enable us to treat each other better.

Speaking of slavery, there exists today a plantation house in Maryland. My friend, Tee, and I rode by the house to see if anyone lived there. To me it looked like a house that was used in a scary movie, it was very eerie. Tee told me it was previously a slave plantation; my curiosity was stroked. A couple of days later, I took a trip there. The house was built in 1746, and it is still standing.

After visiting the plantation house, I knew that I was drawn to it for a reason. Unfortunately, I didn't know exactly why at that time but I had my own reasons and philosophy for the strong attachment to the house. However, on this night a part of my prayer was answered as I stood on the porch of the house and asked God why was I attached to the house? "God, you know that I am not into any witchcraft or anything, so please show me in the name of Jesus." My reason for bringing up witchcraft is that there is said to be restless spirits that haunt this house and people have come forth to tell me different things that have happened to them, or to someone that they knew personally. I've been visiting the house since 2007. Over the years, I have met historians and students of history. The plantation was built in the year 1746. Slave traders would often sell Irish, British, and African American slaves.

It was late spring 2009, a night of routine chores, ironing clothes and carrying out my mommy duties. "Night, night Serenity," was my last verbal communication for the night. Down I went, fast asleep.

THE DREAM

Within seconds, I was at a plantation house; my friends were there with me for a brief second and then disappeared. A black cat ran to the bottom of the house, under the stairs. I was told the cat rarely leaves the property and has been around for a while. Anyway, he ran hurriedly from underneath the house; I knew something was wrong. Out of nowhere, a young girl, maybe early twenties, emerged from the bottom of the house. With outstretched eyes, I couldn't believe what I was seeing.

The girl stretched her body then looked around as if she was lost; she looked like a former slave by the clothes she wore. She looked at me and asked, "What year is this?" I replied, "It is 2009." She said, "I have been asleep for over three-hundred years." I remained calm while fascinated at the same time. With a serious look on her face, she said, "Your name is Lakisha Davis. When you were five-years-old your cousin raped you. You are trying to find your significance in this house. None of your ancestor's lived on this property. I died at a young age and was murdered at this house; my uncle was murdered here too and is buried under this house." The slave girl, at least that is how she appeared, was the same race as me. This slave girl, whom I will name Sara, said, "Don't come back to the plantation house anymore, for your own good." She revealed more to me, but I'll just leave it at that. Her words left me speechless, and I woke up.

When I woke up, it was time to get ready for work, for real. I made it on time.

Months prior to my dream, I took my friend, Ben, on a tour of the plantation. On this night, the college's historical department was sponsoring an event. As we pulled into the driveway, there was a host of cars. We got out of the car and went to the event. I knew the student who resided there, and she gave us permission to tour the house. We walked to the area where the garden used to be. A wooden arch, which was designed as a point of entrance was still in place. We stepped inside the garden. Ben stared with fright in his eyes and backed away. I asked, "What is wrong?" He said, "Please don't think I am crazy but there is a dead young girl by those bushes to the right. She is lying with her arm in front of her and her other arm behind her. Her head is tilted to the side with blood running down her mouth, she has on dirty white clothes, or maybe they are brown. Someone killed her."

He was anxious to leave. As we were walking to the car, he looked backward toward the garden and told me to look up the name Sara. We left. He didn't get a chance to go inside the plantation house, perhaps it wasn't meant for him to.

There have been sightings of restless spirits in the plantation house seen by people who are blessed with the gift of discernment or prophetic insight. These gifts are activated in the spiritual realm causing the person to see beyond the natural realm into the supernatural world. You can read about the gifts of the Spirit in the Bible.

Another sighting in the spiritual world that occurred was when a white woman came through the wall and introduced herself, she wanted to know why there were visitors in the house. From what I was told, the visitors told the woman that she was the caregiver of the house, and they listened; then, she turned around and walked through the wall as if she was on skates.

On another occasion, I was told that two little children were heard laughing and playing while running up and down the steps.

One evening while sitting on the porch of the house, a gentleman came to tend the landscape. I asked him if he ever heard of any mention of restless spirits on the property. He didn't think my question was bizarre. He told me that he and his partner were cutting the grass, and when his partner looked up, he saw a little girl standing in the top window on the side of the house which had the number 1746 carved in it. My reasons for being attached to the house were not what I thought. However, the reason came to me after the dream.

First and foremost, the reason I am sharing these encounters with you is because I want you to know. Secondly, if restless spirits from slavery times are in bondage due to a lack of rest and peace, then what effect do you think mental bondage has on a restless mind? Mental bondage will find a way to occupy your thoughts leaving no room for mental peace or stability.

"Your Deliverance is Coming!"

CHAPTER 7

Breaking Generational Curses & Receiving the Lord's Blessings!

Deuteronomy 28 – Blessings and Cursings

God gave me the passion for freedom, the inquisitiveness to seek the truth about generational blessings and curses and generational gifts that I may confirm its authenticity. Generational curses can be broken through prayer coupled with establishing new behavioral patterns. In our DNA lies the gift of generational blessings. But, curses can be broken, and gifts/blessings untapped from a lack of knowledge. If you do not possess these gifts or even inquire about them, they will go to the grave with you. We all have a purpose here on Earth; that is why we only have a certain amount of time to fulfill our purpose.

I believe centuries ago a curse was formed that wrapped its ugly arms around both sides of my family and squeezed tight. Maybe during slavery, or before slavery began, I know that my bloodline extends beyond my great-grandparents. One of the most dominant curses in my family is the inability to heal from matters of the heart. I witnessed this trait on my mother's side of the family and within myself. The pain lies dormant until it is triggered emotionally. I am speaking from the place of observation of what I saw manifesting when I was fifteen years old.

Because I didn't know my mother's whereabouts, I didn't know who her family was, except my Aunt Gee, who lived in D.C., my mother's sister. The only real family I knew was my Dad's family. One day I decided to visit my Aunt Gee; I hadn't seen her in many years. However, I remembered where she worked as I remembered the last place my mother lived. From the age of four years old until now, I have stored memories of critical things whether good or bad.

During the first visit to my aunt's job, she told me that my Great Uncle Billy, which is my mom's uncle, wanted to meet me. This was our second time seeing each other. I was excited about meeting my uncle and the remainder of my family. When we finally met, I was ecstatic by the number of family members my mother has.

Let me continue!

I met my great Uncle Billy and his wife Aunt Precious when they visited our home on 5th Street. I smiled big as I always did, and embraced them with a hug! I asked if they knew where my mother was because I was looking for her; I believed she was still alive somewhere out there. They didn't have a clue! Out of the blue, I asked them a straightforward question, "Can I live with you because our house need repairs, and I don't want to live here anymore until the repairs are completed?" The nerve of me! I just met them. My Uncle said "yes" and his wife concurred. This was the beginning journey with my mother's family. I was fifteen years old when I moved in and stayed until I graduated from high school. It was the adult thing to do. I didn't want to wear my welcome out.

The first honorable trait I recognize in the Davis' family is that we stick together. Regardless of what went on within the family, being there for another was the foundation. I lived in the house with my aunt and uncle and their three daughters: Tina, Tracey and her husband Terrance, and son; then, Kenya and her son Tee. My aunt and uncle have other children, but they didn't live there. They all are a few years older than me. They always support each other, and they have often supported me, during my prom, wedding, and many other events. I truly appreciate it!

The blessings that I see on my mother's side are the spirit of hard work, having the drive to work, and persevering no matter what. There is no room for laziness, just persistence. I am happy to be connected to the strength within my family. I didn't discover the spiritual gifts within the family because I wasn't aware of spiritual gifts until my early twenties. I had already moved out and was on my own journey.

On my mother's side of the family, the spirits that are operational causing curses are motherly abandonment and rejection. As a result of these curses, there is a yearning for motherly love. I believe my mother wanted it from her mother just as I did from her.

How do I know generational curses are real? I'll put it this way; I am a believer who experienced it for myself. I have yearned deeply for love, wanting someone to take care of me and love me for who I am. I would often see single women looking very happy and free from commitment. However, I felt empty without a man to caress me. I was trying to fill a void, just like my mother had tried to do many times in her life, I am sure. God revealed the root of my dysfunctional relationships that never worked out. He said, "You are under a generational curse, and it is up to you to break it before your children are born." I didn't want to believe it, so I continued to entertain my search for love.

As time passed, God revealed things in the supernatural realm about curses and bondage; the insight was alarming because this information was new to me. Now, I saw clearly, what had transpired in my life over the last seven years. I have been under a curse, as well as in bondage to many things, e.g., sex that gave me a false sense of security. I felt wanted and loved as I lay with another. The more I discovered about myself, the more depressed I became. A war was waged against my flesh and mind and I rebelled. Rebellion and the spirit of self-destruction tormented me day in and day out. What I had to realize is that Satan never sleeps; he is always working. I believe that someone reading this book can relate to the demonic attacks in the mind. I couldn't focus; my energy waned, and my faith weakened as a result. I asked God why He showed me what was going on in my life. I felt if He wasn't going to help me He would not have revealed it to me. From that moment, I felt a thick black cloud over me every day because the exposer to the curse was all over me. I thought about the harm that had been done to me through the years. I had to get control again; I needed rest within my soul, and peace was needed ASAP. I had to lay in Zion (a spiritual resting place) to get some rest.

Mount Zion is a mountain where the prophet Moses visited so he could hear from God. I wasn't able to go there physically, but mentally. I really believe had I not taken the time to meditate, I would not be here today. My mind, body, and emotions struggled to adjust to the revelations I received and to get accustomed to the changes I had to make. Generational curses are in the blood; it is not a learned behavior. Trust me. I know how it feels to want to change things about yourself and nothing changes no matter how hard you try.

In God's lovingkindness, He drew my attention to Him. I realized that I had better take God up on His offer instead of the touch of men or I would never know true happiness otherwise.

The offer:

"Are you tired? Worn out? Burned out on religion? Come to me. Get away with me and you'll recover your life. I'll show you how to take a real rest. Walk with me and work with me—watch how I do it. Learn the unforced rhythms of grace. I won't lay anything heavy or ill-fitting on you. Keep company with me and you'll learn to live freely and lightly."—Matthew 11:28-30

This is how God showed his love for us: God sent his only Son into the world so we might live through Him. This is the kind of love we are talking about—not that we once upon a time loved God, but that He loved us and sent his Son as a sacrifice to clear away our sins and the damage they've done to our relationship with God.— 1 John 4:9

He showed me true and everlasting love; love that is unbreakable, a love that will never abandon you. Yes! God is love! No other love pleased me no matter how hard I tried to believe that I felt loved. God wanted me to love Him first and then love me. When I began loving me, I felt and looked different. I beamed with radiance. Love was looking for me and found me. Praise God, the Creator, for loving you and creating you. He is a mighty God!

Give thanks to the Lord, for he is good;
His love endures forever.—1 Chronicles 16:34 (NIV)

By identifying with the power of touch as a mom, I believe every motherly touch leads us to Jesus. God is a Spirit, but His touch is real and powerful, I can feel His touch deep down in my heart. Once I realized that God was all I needed, He sent me a helpmate, someone to physically care for me and touch me. The curse was broken. *Wow!* Generational curses that entered through my ancestors, were passed down from generation to generation. I am glad God used me to discover them and break its power. I prayed for all curses knowingly or unknowingly in my bloodline to be broken, in the name of Jesus. In retrospect, I appreciate the family meetings my great Uncle Billy had because they enlightened me about my family's history and me.

Some people really don't believe in generational curses but believe it is from the devil or witchcraft. In my opinion, curses can come upon families because of disobedience. Yes, there are people who practice evil, but I am referring to curses that follow your descendants, e.g. diabetes, high blood pressure and many other illnesses that were transferred through the bloodline, the ancestral DNA.

God speaks about curses in the Bible (Deuteronomy 28th chapter), and how they can come upon generations of people. The Bible also references topics, i.e., angels, demons, healing, lust, and many others, which have influenced families. Everything that we experience have been experienced long ago, before we were born. Therefore, I believe there is hope and a future for my family and yours. Just like Dr. Fabulous told me, I have to slay the demons head and show my daughter how to do it to protect her children from the curses put over my family. Thank you Dr. Fabulous.

When I mention the word curse, some people are prepared to hear the worst, but it is a part of life. Unfortunately, I have to endure the hardships that come along while writing this chapter because of the seriousness of this particular issue. It can be stressful at times, particularly when I think of the pain and emotions of my past. I used to be critical of myself. Failure has prevented me, in some aspect, of believing that my dreams can't come to fruition. I looked at my dreams from a distance, though they were near. Yet, I have faith that God will complete the work He started within me, and I have confidence that I will do my part.

I now understand why God chose me to write a book on deliverance. What the enemy meant for evil, God will turn it around for good.

As far as I am concerned, God turned into good what you meant for evil, for He brought me to this high position I have today so that I could save the lives of many people.—Gen. 50:20 (TLB)

I am smiling as I write this book, because I know that it will help many others. One of the many gifts that I believe God has given me is Faith. God always reminds me of His promises. He promised me that if I trust Him in everything that I will be just fine in every area of my life.

After addressing curses, I will now switch the frequency. But whatever you do, please stay tuned because there's more to come.

Gifts from God, our Creator!

He has so many gifts to give us, if only we would accept them. Some people die with their gifts trapped inside of them, ones they never used. There are also unique gifts called "generational gifts." These can be recognized in families. Have you ever noticed within a family that each one can sing? Not only can they sing, but their ancestors too, so you were told. When you don't tap into your gift it will lie dormant within you. The reason could be because there are too many distractions or perhaps a lack of knowledge concerning your gifts.

Thank you Lord for giving me the desire to know who I am and the knowledge and discernment to understand all you have imparted within me. Thank you Lord for everything that has to do with me. Lord, please open up the ears and hearts of everyone reading this book. Let no one, not another soul leave this Earth with their gifts trapped inside them. In Jesus Name, Amen!

Now, there is substantial evidence that I have discovered within me and my Dad's family. We are intertwined in more ways than one. I have been around them my entire life, so I say this with confidence and assurance. The first trait I noticed is we have faith, the size of a watermelon, greater than the size of mustard seed faith as mentioned in the Bible (Matthew 17:20). Our faith in God has grown to such a level based on what we have seen Him do in our lives. Although we have never physically seen Him, we feel His spirit. It is similar to the feeling people feel in the spirit of music as you're being led by the rhythm. The seed of faith was planted in three generations. Reader believe that God can do anything but fail!

One day, Tonya and I were leaving her house. I lived with her after leaving an abusive relationship. I prayed to God to provide a way of escape, and she prayed for me too. Thanks! Anyway, we were leaving for work and just before she locked the door behind us, Tonya said "Daddy (in reference to God) I need some money, I am broke! As we walked out the gate onto the sidewalk, Tonya looked down and saw a twenty dollar bill. I couldn't believe it, then again I could. God gave His baby some lunch money. I laughed and looked up to the sky and said "Lord what about me?" Tonya, my lovely cousin whom I love with all my heart, lost her sight over seven years ago. She refused to allow her physical challenges get the best of her. Accompanied by her blind stick, she completed school and was one of the first blind students who graduated from Maryland University College, in College Park Maryland, with her

Bachelors in Computer Studies. Let me tell you, I was screaming as if I were at a football game. I know it was her faith that allowed her to move mountains of fear or self-doubt as she persevered and claimed her victory as she walked across the stage. Hallelujah!

My Dad's faith is powerful too. His faith ignites my faith. He knows for a fact that God alone is a way maker. When man has exhausted all possibilities, God can do the impossible. In Hebrews 11th chapter, we read about great people of faith who believed God against all odds. Do you have faith? Are you facing an insurmountable problem and it looks like the odds are stacked against you? NOTHING is too hard for God! He makes the impossible, possible. In Jesus name!

My Dad taught me that if you believe you will receive. Faith without works is useless, meaning you can have faith but if you don't step forward and take the first step, your faith will not be manifested in the Earth. We have faith; we believe the best in the worst situations. Having faith is not an easy task. Especially when the odds are against you and everything around you looks dark and gloomy! There is hope!

My Dad had faith that God would take care of me and heal my mind after being raped. God has been carrying me. My Dad has faith that he will live and not die until all of his assignments on this Earth is completed. On various occasions, the spirit of death came to take my Dad away, but our combined faith as a family fought against the death angel. We are a praying family because we believe in the power of prayer. In 2013, Tonya summoned an emergency family prayer telephone conference. We utilized the three–way call feature and the speakerphone. We were able to call one of her brother's in Florida. My husband witnessed this electrifying night as he participated in prayer with his new family.

From generation to generation, the gift of faith has been passed down. What a remarkable discovery! This makes my heart smile. You learn a lot about people and life when you pay attention.

I have noticed how Serenity has already been touched by the gift. Prayer is part of her life, and she does it every night. She understands that God is the source to every living thing she sees. When she was six years old, I asked her once if she thought someone made water and poured it into the ocean with a bucket. Only God can do something like that I explained. I further commented on how the stars stretch across the sky, nothing holds them up there and keep them in place. God is real! My baby's faith is so amazing. Just a few days before she said "Mommy I asked God to let it snow, look outside. I knew that He was going to do it Mommy." I looked at her and smiled because I am so happy to know that my daughter has embraced her gift at an early age.

Another gift I discovered is the ability to dream, dreams that have come to pass in reality. Visions are another gift, which my cousin Kevin terms "déjà vu." At the end of last year, my Dad shared a dream with me which came to past. Tomorrow, when we take him to dinner we'll unfold the mystery. This is a wonderful gift to have when you see good things, but when the dreams aren't so pleasant, it becomes a hard pill to swallow at the moment.

THE DREAM

I had a dream about the D.C sniper before he started his killing spree. In my dream, I was in a neighborhood that was shaped like a "U." There was one way in and one way out. I was sitting up high as if I was sitting in the sky looking down. A Caprice pulled up with two men in it, and they started shooting at everybody, older people, kids, anybody in their sight. I woke up in disbelief; I shook it off and didn't think any more about it until months later when I saw the story flashing across the news. I don't think my dream occurred in the same year of the incident. In my dreams the scenario is the same but the surrounding environment and people are often different in reality. When everyone was on a sniper watch, I remembered the dream and wasn't afraid for some reason. While travelling on the T18 bus from New Carrollton subway station, we were instructed not to sit next to windows but I did. I believe God showed me that dream to beware but also to give me a heads up on the signs of the time. The end! All types of foolishness will trigger during this period and I see it! I had a dream about the Tsunami. I didn't know it at the time, but I was somewhere in mid-air, not too high up but not on ground level. I saw water swallowing houses and all kinds of fish were coming up and out of the water. The fish were tropical, and there were some fish that I have never seen with my eyes before. All of a sudden, I saw a buddy of mine, Keith, at the top of a tree holding on for dear life as the tree swung back and forth. He saw me and began yelling for help, but I couldn't help him. I woke up!

THE DREAM

I met First Lady Michelle Obama, and I was talking to her about Life Without My Mother (Chapter 1). She was so laid back and cool with her advice to me. I felt drawn to her because she is a mother and a very strong woman.

Let's see together if this dream comes true.

Sometime later, I saw the Tsunami and what happened there but the fish were a reminder of the dream that I had. So I am a believer in the gifts that my family possess. I was also given confirmation by a prophetic woman I didn't even know concerning my spiritual gifts. She was a prophet for sure because she told me about things that I did in my private life when no one was around. When she spoke of the gifts God gave me I was in shock but they started manifesting themselves within me and I embraced them.

I would like to share with you something that I see within my Dad's bloodline. My Grandfather Willie Norman was born in 1895, in a town called Edgefield South Carolina, the same year Frederick Douglas died in Washington, D.C., a city he lived in. How ironic? I toured his house and stood at the bottom of the steps where he took his last breath.

My Grandfather Willie Norman had two sons, Rudolph Norman and Horace Norman, and one daughter Willie Lee Norman, who was birthed by my grandmother—his second wife. My Dad's siblings and their children, including me, lived together in the same house. I was the youngest cousin in the house but not for long. Two babies were born into our family, Kevin & Kervin, sons of my cousin Kevin. When you visit my website, you will see them both in my documentary "Kevin & Kervin." There are certain character traits that I see in Kervin which remind me of my Dad. I also believe they can be traced back to Willie Norman. I wish I could tell you more but I can't! My grandfather had other children from his previous marriage. He was twenty-four years older than my grandma. I will address his life, prior to moving to Washington D.C based on the information given to me. So here I am, Lakisha Norman Davis the offspring of my grandfather. He died before I was able to talk but he did get the opportunity to see me. When I hear stories about him I feel his spirit all over me. Let me explain, my grandfather grew up during an era when you could not look white people in their face; you would get lynched. He witnessed these events. He vowed that when he moved north he would live in a predominantly black community. When he spoke to people he never looked away. He demanded the same respect from his children—look him in the face while talking to him; this was a sign of respect and confidence. My Dad has adopted the same philosophy. He will view you in a different light if you do not make eye contact with him while speaking. I agree with their philosophy. When I talk to people, I look them in their face. If the courtesy is not extended I feel disrespected, or think they have something to hide. I also feel as if I am wasting my time due to a lack of conversations. Must I engage in a conversation by myself? I don't know if this trait is a blessing or curse, I do know it has been transferred through our bloodline. There are other unmentionable traits I learned surrounding the birth of my grandfather. Due to reasons of being misunderstood, me and my family, I'll refrain from further discussion. The residue and pain of the south affected my grandfather. He became a man of few words and positive action while maintaining a very strong personality. I must admit I am not a woman of few words. However, when I am concentrating or strategizing my goals, this trait is emphasized.

So let me tell you now the curses that I have discovered on my Dad's side. The spirit of gluttony, the enjoyment of over indulging in food but people can be a glutton for many other things. I have noticed three generations of my family members who suffer with sugar diabetes. Beginning at the age of fourteen years old until today, I have traveled back and forth to the hospital with my Dad regarding sugar diabetes complications. I have spoken with many doctors regarding my Dad's health, and I know the proper medical terms for many of my Dad's issues. There are two doctors whom I respect highly, and they respect me for caring for my Dad. One is at Howard University Hospital, he has been attending to my Dad's care for years, the other doctor works at Washington Hospital Center. They both know who they are. Thank you for everything and going beyond the title "Doctor" and really caring for my Dad as if he were your own family member.

Do you know food can really hurt you if not eaten properly? I didn't know it was that serious in the beginning of my life, and now I am fighting for the health of myself and my daughter. We love some good food. It is an unhealthy practice to overindulge or eat foods that may not be good for your body. What's good for one person may not be good for others. This is an ongoing fight which I have been battling for years. My daughter has been born into this curse and now it is up to me to slay the monster called gluttony, set his head on the mantel and show my daughter how to conquer it. Thanks Dr. Fabulous for teaching me about evil spirits, in this case gluttony, through your exemplary efforts. I have fought the spirit many times, some battles I won hands down and others I got my butt kicked. Now I must do what is necessary to prevent gluttony from attacking Serenity's children. My deliverance is coming, in Jesus mighty name! Amen!

I would like to share a power principle with you: receive the Lord's blessing and fight to get rid of the curses by praying, fasting, reading your word and having faith that God will move that mountain in your family's way!

One day in the summer of August 2001 before 9/11 happened, I was waiting for my friend Egypt to pick me up from the Anacostia subway station. We planned to attend Bible Study. As I waited, a young man who appeared to be physically disabled walked by and shouted "girl! A girl"! His speech was slurred, and I felt irritated because he wouldn't stop shouting "A girl" until I acknowledged him. "Yes," I replied. He said, "Hi, my name is Psycho." I said, "Psycho is not your name." He said, "That is my street name. I used to do crazy stuff out here in these streets." I asked, "What happened to you, your body?" He said, "I got hit by an eighteen-wheeler. This is why I am in this condition." He proceeded to tell me that he grew up in church, and Lucifer wanted him to bow down and totally join his side since he was already doing devilish things in the street. He said when he refused the offer, out of nowhere an eighteen-wheeler truck struck him, and left his body deformed. He said, "Lakisha the war of Armageddon is near, and people are going to die and lose their homes, but as for you God said that he got you!" I told him that I battle with sins and felt bad about it, so I was wondering if God was mad at me! He wasn't I see! Egypt pulled up, and I got in the car. When I looked back at the man named Psycho, his eyes were shining bright like the sun! Egypt and I drove off; I told her everything that just happened. Egypt and my other friend Delshaun often studied the Book of Revelation. Revelation teaches on the end times. I believe what it says particularly regarding the changing of seasons. On Sunday, February 23, 2014, it felt like a nice spring day, and on Tuesday, February 25, 2014, it snowed. God said that you would know when the end is near when you can't distinguish the seasons. There are many signs of the end time. Check out the Book of Revelation, Daniel, and Timothy which reference the last days too. There you will gain insight and understanding of the end times.

A blessing from God

One Friday night, DelShaun and I went to the store. I remember it just as clear as I see the paper I am writing on. There was a lady in line who appeared to be in her mid to late forties. She looked troubled to say the least. Out of nowhere, two young ladies began harassing her for no reason. DelShaun intervened and said, "Leave her alone, pick with me!" After her comment, I knew this was going to be a long night. I couldn't let my girl go out like that. We came to the store together and we were going to leave together. Period! We didn't know the outcome, but God did. DelShaun put her life on the line, as great leaders have in the past, for the wellbeing of others. The two young ladies retreated. They preyed on the weak and God used Delshaun to aid in her defense. For safety purposes, we walked the lady to the corner; she cried along the way. While trying to console her, she said that her son was killed by gunshot wounds to his head. My heart sank, and so did DelShaun, who has teenage boys.

DelShaun and I prayed for her. DelShaun prayed so loud I am sure people could hear her for blocks away. There was power behind her prayer and you could feel it. I felt like I was with John the Baptist; he too shouted in the streets "Repent, Repent for the Kingdom of God is near!"— *Matthew 3:2* (KJV) After the prayer, the lady stopped crying. She told us God prepared her for this moment, and she felt her burdens lifted. She began to glorify God! Amazing!

The gears shift. DelShaun and I began walking. It was dark outside. We heard some church music playing next to a Chinese carryout. The church looked like a store front church. I asked DelShaun if she wanted to go in; curiosity got the best of me. She agreed! When we sat down, DelShaun grabbed a Bible and started flipping through the pages. The Holy Spirit led me to move and sit behind the deacon. I handed him a note that I had just written. "I said that I had something to tell the church!" The deacon handed the note to the pastor and low and behold, he let me speak in the pulpit! I said, "The end is near!" God want us to be ready for His return." I said more, but it was the Holy Spirit speaking through me.

All of a sudden, this lady in the church got up and started dancing very provocatively. The pastor and his deacons surrounded her, got some Holy oil and started praying for her. They sensed a lustful demon on her and I couldn't agree more. It was like a scene in a movie. Someone began speaking in tongues, and that is when DelShaun wrote a note to the pastor. She said that no one should speak in tongues according to the Word unless there is an interpreter because they could be speaking in a devilish tongue and we left the church.

This chapter ends with this story because one of the greatest gifts from God you could ever receive is the Gift of the Holy Spirit! Receive Him if you have not and allow Him to catapult you into new dimensions of the Divine.

The stage is set; this is my life story, but it doesn't end here. Be encouraged as you read and memorize the prayer of Serenity.

"God grant me the Serenity to accept the things I cannot change, courage to change the things I can, and wisdom to know the difference."

American theologian Reinhold Niebuhr (1892–1971).

ABOUT THE AUTHOR

Lakisha is a young woman from the historical inner city area of Shaw, Washington, D.C.

For over eighteen years, she served in the capacity of administration for the Federal Government. Her passion for writing began at an early age. As a result, she gained a love for writing poetry, which has landed her in prestigious places. Lakisha is also an actor who displays her talents in stage plays and community events.

Lakisha serves as Vice President of the Lakeisha Brown Foundation (LBF), where she is able to offer a voice of change that influences those around her. As an advocate for rape victims and domestic violence, she has helped women improve their lives by engaging in prayer, consultation, and crisis management.

In addition to her other roles, she is an author, wife, mother, motivational speaker, and a leader in her community.

Your Deliverance is Coming Journal

For the next 30 days, think and write about your healing process, the successes and challenges you face in deliverance/healing. At the conclusion of the thirty-day cycle, please send a testimonial of your progress, if this book has been helpful to you. We would love to hear from you.

Please visit www.lakishadavissmall.com or
Email: lakishadavissmall@gmail.com

Day 1

Day 2

Day 3

Day 4

Day 5

Day 6

Day 7

Day 8

Day 9

Day 10

Day 11

Day 12

Day 13

Day 14

Day 15

Day 16

Day 17

Day 18

Day 19

Day 20

Day 21

Day 22

Day 23

Day 24

Day 25

Day 26

Day 27

Day 28

Day 29

Day 30